MW01601170

NORTH CAROLINA
DRIVER HANDBOOK

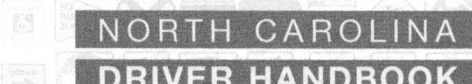

North Carolina Division of Motor Vehicles

Motor vehicle laws and fees are subject to change by the North Carolina General Assembly. Revised April 2018. Current fees effective January 1, 2016.

The North Carolina Driver Handbook is available online at **MyNCDMV.gov** under License and ID.

Division of Motor Vehicles
Driver and Vehicle Services Section
North Carolina Transportation

Physical Location: (DMV Headquarters)
(Licenses are not issued at this location).
1100 New Bern Avenue, Raleigh, NC 27697

Mailing Address:
3123 Mail Service Center
Raleigh, NC 27697-3123

MyNCDMV.gov

200,000 copies of this publication were printed at a cost of $58,917.60 or $0.29 a copy. (4/2018)

North Carolina Division of Motor Vehicles

Dear North Carolina Driver:

Earning your North Carolina driver license can help you travel to places of uncommon beauty and diversity across our state. It also comes with the added responsibility of following the rules of the road to protect your fellow travelers.

You'll be joining more than 7.4 million licensed drivers throughout the state. When you are behind the wheel, we count on you to drive safely and look out for others. By taking driving safety seriously, you can help reduce the 300,000 crashes and more than 1,400 fatalities on our highways each year.

This handbook was written to help prepare you for your driver license examination. It offers valuable safe driving techniques to help keep you out of harm's way. If you need additional assistance, contact your nearest driver license office or go online to MyNCDMV.gov.

Best wishes for safe driving,

Roy Cooper
Governor

James H. Trogdon, III
Secretary of Transportation

North Carolina Division of Motor Vehicles

Dear North Carolina Driver:

When you earn the privilege of driving in North Carolina, you are responsible for your life and the lives of others who travel our streets, roads and highways. It is up to each of us who drive a vehicle to protect the millions of citizens who travel the same roads, whether by car, truck, motorcycle, bicycle or foot.

Please use this driver handbook to learn and reinforce your safe and defensive driving techniques. Make yourself familiar with the motor vehicle laws of our state and the ways you can improve your driving.

As you prepare for the driver license examination, we invite you to contact DMV or your nearest driver license office for additional assistance. You can find the locations of North Carolina driver license offices and other helpful information on our website at MyNCDMV.gov.

Remember, always drive safely and obey the rules of the road. With your help, we can keep North Carolina's roadways safe.

Sincerely,

Torre J. Jessup
Commissioner of Motor Vehicles

DMV *directAccess*
automated information by telephone

DMV*directAccess* is a convenient way to obtain information about driver licenses and vehicle registration from the North Carolina Department of Transportation (NCDOT) Division of Motor Vehicles (DMV). Dial (919) 715-7000 from a touch-tone telephone, and access information 24 hours a day, seven days a week.

DMV*directAccess* gives you the facts about:

• Driver licenses, learner permits, motorcycle license endorsements, commercial driver licenses (CDLs) and special identification cards;

• Personalized information you should know about points against your driver license, your driving record and the status of your driver license;

• Medical and vision forms, exam cycles, records and hearings;

• Vehicle registration, duplicate titles, lost or stolen license plates, personalized and vanity license plates and handicapped placards; and

• Liability insurance and more.

DMV*directAccess* also includes information about driver license and vehicle registration taxes and fees. By entering your zip code, the system can give you the location of a driver license or vehicle registration office in your area.

DMV Information (919) 715-7000

Other DMV Telephone Listings:

Traffic Records Section. . . . . (919) 615-6131

International Registration Plan (IRP) Section . . . . (919) 615-6700

Tag and Tax Together. . . . . (919) 814-1779

DMV on the Web   *MyNCDMV.gov*

The NCDMV website focuses on providing North Carolina's motorists with timely and accurate information regarding NCDMV services and issues. The site answers your most frequently asked questions and includes up-to-date directories of all DMV offices statewide. You will also find news about new legislation and other requirements affecting North Carolina motorists. Publications and forms are also available online.

Duplicate Driver License/Duplicate Identification Card on the Web

A duplicate driver license/duplicate identification card may be requested online at *MyNCDMV.gov*, provided that DMV has your last image on file and a valid social security number or a document issued by the United States government indicating legal presence. A duplicate driver license/identification card may be requested for the following reasons:

• To replace a lost or stolen license/identification card;

• To change a residence and/or mailing address; or

• To replace a license/identification card that is defaced or damaged.

A fee of $13 is charged and may be paid with any credit or debit card. A duplicate license/identification card with the most recent photo available in our computer system will be mailed to the customer.

Online Renewal

The online driver license process is available to drivers every other time they renew their license, which is allowed up to six months before its expiration date. It is a process that should take just a few minutes, as a customer goes to the DMV online webpage, and uses the appropriate link under the Drivers section.

Drivers must verify their identity, confirm they live at the address on the license, and have no vision problems that would hinder their driving skills, and that all the statements being given are truthful. They also must have their current driver license number to complete the online form and a major credit card or debit card to pay for the renewal. The new license will be mailed in 7-14 business days, and will be valid for 5 or 8 years, depending on the driver's age.

Customers cannot use the online system to obtain first time licenses or ID cards. This also applies to first time REAL ID issuances. Online service is also not available if a driver has a restriction other than corrective lenses on their license, is in the medical review program, is trying to renew a commercial driver license or a state ID card, or has an expired suspended or revoked license. Those customers must still complete those processes at a DMV license office.

Transportation Alternatives

For many North Carolinians, operating a vehicle may be too costly, inconvenient or dangerous. The North Carolina Department of Transportation wants you to know there are many transportation alternatives to driving. In our society, we often overlook our options to walk, ride a bicycle, carpool and use public transportation.

Public transportation could be your best alternative to driving. Some form of public transportation is available in most areas of the state. In the larger metropolitan areas, there are bus systems that operate on regular routes. Smaller rural areas may provide coordinated van services for citizens. In either case, public transportation is available and equipped to accommodate persons with disabilities.

To learn more about public transportation options in your area, call:

N.C. Department of Transportation
Public Transportation Division
(919) 733-4713

Chapter 1
Your License

Driving is a legal privilege and responsibility. It is against the law to drive a motor vehicle on streets and highways without a valid driver license. It is also illegal to sit in the driver's seat of a motor vehicle while the engine is running or to steer a motor vehicle while it is being pushed or towed by another vehicle if you do not have a valid driver license.

Office Hours

Driver license examiners throughout the state are trained to test fairly and to give prompt and courteous service. Most offices offer services from 8:00 a.m. to 5:00 p.m. In larger cities and towns, the offices are open Monday through Friday, and some are open Saturday mornings. Offices in smaller towns may only be open for certain days each week. Appointments for driver license examinations can be made by contacting your local driver license office. For an up to date list of office hours and locations, please visit *MyNCDMV.gov*

> **For an original driver license of any type, you may be tested on:**
> - Vision;
> - Knowledge of motor vehicle laws;
> - Traffic signs; and
> - Driving skill (on-road test).

Learner Permit

- Learner permits are available to persons age 18 and older.
- A learner permit authorizes the permit holder to drive a specified type or class of motor vehicle while in possession of the permit.
- The permit holder must, while operating a motor vehicle over the highways, be accompanied by a person who is licensed to operate the motor vehicle being driven and is seated beside the permit holder.
- Required testing includes vision, traffic signs, and knowledge of motor vehicle laws.

Motorcycle Learner Permit

- If an applicant is at least 16 years old but less than 18 years old, the applicant must possess a full provisional license issued by the division. Parent or guardian's signature is required.
- If an applicant is 18 years old or older, the applicant must possess a license issued by the division.
- The motorcycle learner permit authorizes a person to operate a motorcycle without passengers.
- If an applicant is less than 18 years old, the applicant must successfully complete the Motorcycle Safety Foundation Basic Rider Course or the North Carolina Motorcycle Safety Education Program Basic Rider Course.

- The motorcycle learner permit is valid for 12 months and may be renewed for one additional six-month period.
- Required testing includes vision, traffic signs, and the motorcycle knowledge test.

Each driver license test must be passed separately. Applicants for a CDL Class A, B or C license should study the required chapters of the *CDL Handbook*. Applicants for a motorcycle endorsement or motorcycle learner permit should study the *Motorcycle Handbook*. The *CDL Handbook* is available from the Federal Motor Carrier Safety Administration. You may also obtain the CDL, Regular and Motorcycle handbooks on the DMV website and at the local driver license offices. Visit the DMV website at *MyNCDMV.gov*.

Test Requirements for an Original Driver License

Vision
Whether you are applying for a learner permit, an original license or a renewal license in person, your vision must be checked to see that you meet certain standards. If you need corrective lenses to bring your vision up to the required standards, you must wear the lenses at all times while driving and your license will indicate a restriction that you must wear corrective lenses. The penalty for driving without the proper corrective lenses is the same as driving without a license.

Traffic Signs
All the information on the traffic signs test is in this handbook. To pass the signs test, you must identify the traffic signs by color and shape and explain what each means.

Knowledge Test
The knowledge test is about traffic laws and safe driving practices. Audio tests are available, upon request, for those who have difficulty reading.

Driving Skills
The driving test is an on-the-road demonstration of your driving ability. You must perform this test after you have passed all the other tests. The first time you apply for a license, you must take the driving test. You might also have to take it to renew your license. It is not required for a learner permit.

During the on-the-road test, you will be given an opportunity to perform basic driving patterns and to show your ability to drive safely with traffic.

Health Requirements
Individuals may not be licensed if they suffer from a mental or physical condition that might keep them from driving safely. A person with a disability may be issued a restricted license provided the condition does not keep them from driving safely.

Skills observed and graded during the on-the-road driving test:

- Approaches to intersections, stop signs and traffic signals;
- Quick stops — stopping as quickly and safely as possible when told to do so;
- Backing;
- Stopping, starting and parking;
- Use of the clutch (in vehicles with standard transmissions);
- Turn signals and use of the horn;
- Turning;
- Use of lanes;
- Following another vehicle;
- Passing and being passed;
- Yielding the right of way to pedestrians and other vehicles;
- Driving posture; and
- Three-point turnabout.

Applicants for an original driver license must take the on-the-road driving test; however, there are some cases when the on-the-road test may not be required.

Types of Licenses, Permits and Restrictions

North Carolina has a regular driver license and a commercial driver license (CDL). The type of vehicle you will operate determines the class of driver license you must have and the type vehicle in which you must take the driving skills test. The driving skills test must be performed in a vehicle representative of the class license desired.

> **TIP**
>
> *Three-Point Turnabout*
>
> (1) Start from the extreme right side of the road. Look for other traffic and if clear, give a left signal and proceed forward slowly while turning the steering wheel to the left. Stop within several inches of the left curb or edge of the street.
>
> (2) Then proceed backward slowly while turning the steering wheel to the right. Stop within several inches of the right curb or edge of the street.
>
> (3) Proceed forward slowly while turning the steering wheel to the left. This should complete your turnabout.

Regular Licenses

Class A: Required to operate a combination of vehicles that is exempt from CDL requirements when the towed unit has a gross vehicle weight rating (GVWR) of 10,001 pounds or more.

Class B: Required to operate any single vehicle that is exempt from CDL requirements with a GVWR of 26,001 pounds or more, and any such vehicle towing a vehicle with a GVWR not in excess of 10,000 pounds.

Class C: Required to operate any noncommercial single vehicle with a GVWR of less than 26,001 pounds; and a vehicle towing a vehicle which has a combined GVWR of less than 26,001 pounds operated by a driver 18 years old or older. *Most drivers need only a Regular Class C license to operate personal automobiles and small trucks.*

Commercial Driver License (CDL)

A CDL is required for drivers, paid or volunteer, who drive the following types of vehicles that are designed or used to transport passengers or property:

Class A Motor Vehicle: A vehicle that has a combined GVWR of at least 26,001 pounds and includes as part of the combination a towed unit that has a GVWR of at least 10,001 pounds.

Class B Motor Vehicle:

• A single motor vehicle that has a GVWR of at least 26,001 pounds.

• A combination of motor vehicles that includes as part of the combination a towing unit that has a GVWR of at least 26,001 pounds and a towed unit that has a GVWR of less than 10,001 pounds.

Class C Motor Vehicle: A single or combination of motor vehicles not included in Class A or B but meets any of the following descriptions:

• Is designed to transport 16 or more passengers, including the driver; and

• Is transporting hazardous materials and is required to be placarded.

You do not need a CDL to drive recreational vehicles, military equipment, fire and/or emergency equipment or certain farm vehicles. However, a regular license of the appropriate class is required at all times.

A volunteer member of a fire department, rescue or emergency service (EMS) in the performance of duty may operate a Class A, B or C fire-fighting, rescue or EMS vehicle, or combination of these vehicles while holding either a "Regular" A, B or C License.

A special CDL endorsement is required to haul hazardous materials, transport passengers, drive school buses and school activity buses, pull double trailers or drive tank vehicles. Additional information is in the *CDL Handbook.*

Endorsements

Motorcycle

A person must have a regular or commercial license with a motorcycle endorsement or a motorcycle learner permit before being entitled to operate a motorcycle on public roads.

School Bus/School Activity Bus

The driver of a school bus must be at least 18 years of age, have at least six months driving experience and hold either a Class B or Class C CDL with an "S" (school bus) and a "P" (passenger) endorsement along with a School Bus Driver's Certificate. To obtain a School Bus Driver's Certificate, a person must be specially trained and pass an examination administered by a Driver Education Program Specialist which demonstrates the fitness and competency required to operate the bus. The requirements for a driver of a public school activity bus are the same. The requirements for the driver of a school activity bus are the same except a School Bus Driver's Certificate is not required.

NOTE: *Pursuant to G.S. 20-37.14A, the Division shall not issue or renew a commercial driver license reflecting a "P" or "S" endorsement to anyone required to register under sex offender and public protection registration programs.*

Graduated Licensing—Licensing for Drivers 15–18

Limited Learner Permit

If you are at least 15 years of age and have completed an approved driver education course that meets North Carolina requirements and can present a Driving Eligibility Certificate (issued by the public school system), or a high school diploma or its equivalent, you may apply for a Level One Limited Learner Permit to operate vehicles requiring a Class C License.

- You must be at least 15 years old but less than 18 years old and reside in North Carolina.

- You must present a certificate showing you have passed an approved driver education course consisting of at least 30 hours classroom instruction and six hours behind-the wheel instruction that meets North Carolina requirements before you can take the test for a learner permit.

- You must pass written, sign and vision tests.

- During the first six months, a level one permit authorizes you to drive between the hours of 5 a.m. and 9 p.m., while accompanied by your supervising driver.

- Six months from level one issuance, you are eligible to drive anytime with a supervising driver.

- You must hold this permit for 12 months prior to applying for a Limited Provisional License.

- You will be given a Driving Log to be completed detailing a minimum of 60 hours of operation. Daytime or daylight driving can be performed from sunrise to sunset and as long as daylight exists. Nighttime or night driving can be performed after sunset and within the hours that sunlight or daylight does not exist.

- All passengers must be restrained by seat belt or child safety seat.

- No one except the driver and the supervising driver are allowed in the front seat.

- You are not permitted to use a cell phone or other additional technology associated with a cell phone while operating a motor vehicle on a public street or highway or public vehicular area. Exception: You can use it to call the following regarding an emergency situation: an emergency response operator; a hospital, physician's office or a health clinic; a public or privately owned ambulance company or service; a fire department; a law enforcement agency; your parent, legal guardian or spouse.

NOTE: *Before graduating to level two, you must have no convictions of motor vehicle moving violations, seat belt or cell phone infractions within the preceding six months.*

SUPERVISING DRIVER: *A supervising driver must be a parent, grandparent or guardian of the permit/license holder, or a responsible person approved by the parent or guardian. A supervising driver must hold a valid driver license and must have been licensed for at least five years.*

Level Two Limited Provisional License
- Drivers must be at least 16 years old, but less than 18.

- You may drive without supervision from 5 a.m. until 9 p.m. and at any time when driving directly to or from work or any volunteer fire, rescue or emergency medical service, if you are a member.

- You must hold this license at least six months prior to applying for a Full Provisional License.

- You will be given a Driving Log to be completed detailing a minimum of 12 hours of operation. At least six hours must occur during nighttime hours. Daytime or daylight driving can be performed from sunrise to sunset and as long as daylight exists. Nighttime or night driving can be performed after sunset and within the hours that sunlight or daylight does not exist. The log must be signed by the supervising driver and submitted to the Division at the time of application for the Full Provisional License.

- All passengers must be restrained by seat belt or child safety seat.

- Supervising driver must be seated beside the driver.

- The number of passengers allowed in the vehicle under the age of 21 is restricted to ONE when the driver of the vehicle is the holder of a level II, OR if all passengers under the age of 21 are members of the driver's immediate family or members of the same household as the driver, there is no "under 21" limit. If the supervising driver is in the car, this restriction does not apply.

- You are not permitted to use a cell phone or other additional technology associated with a cell phone while operating a motor vehicle on a public street or highway or public vehicular area. Exception: You can use it to call the following regarding an emergency situation: an emergency response operator; a hospital, physician's office, or a health clinic; a public or privately owned ambulance company or service; a fire department; a law enforcement agency; your parent, legal guardian or spouse.

NOTE: *Before graduating to level three, you must have no convictions of motor vehicle moving violations, seat belt or cell phone infractions within the preceding six months.*

SUPERVISING DRIVER: *A supervising driver must be a parent, grandparent or guardian of the permit/license holder, or a responsible person approved by the parent or guardian. A supervising driver must hold a valid driver license and must have been licensed for at least five years.*

Level Three Full Provisional License
- The restrictions on level one and level two concerning time of driving, supervision and passenger limitations do not apply to a Full Provisional License.

- If you are under the age of 18, you are not permitted to use a cell phone or other additional technology associated with a cell phone while operating a motor vehicle on a public street or highway or public vehicular area. Exception: You can use it to call the following regarding an emergency situation: an emergency response operator; a hospital, physician's office, or a health clinic; a public or privately owned ambulance company or service; a fire department; or a law enforcement agency; your parent, legal guardian or spouse.

New Residents Between the Ages of 15 and 18 Years

If you are a new resident moving into North Carolina and are 15 but less than 18 years old and have a learner permit, a restricted license or an unrestricted license, you should contact your local driver license office to determine which type of license or learner permit you are eligible to apply for.

The Provisional Licensee

Drivers under age 18 are provisional licensees. Because these drivers have a much higher crash rate, special laws apply to them. If you are a driver under age 18:

• You must present a certificate showing you have passed an approved driver education course consisting of at least 30 hours classroom instruction and six hours behind-the-wheel instruction that meets North Carolina requirements before you can take the test for a learner permit or license.

• The DMV reviews your driving record more closely and may contact you if you have certain types of traffic convictions or crashes.

• It is unlawful for a provisional licensee to drive a motor vehicle after or while consuming any amount of alcohol or drugs — a conviction of such a violation will result in a one-year license revocation.

• A parent or legal guardian must sign for a minor.

• You are not permitted to use a cellphone.

• You are not permitted to operate a vehicle while manually entering multiple letters or text as a means of communicating or read any electronic mail or text message.

• Every person occupying a vehicle in motion must have a safety belt properly fastened when the vehicle is in motion.

Thinking Of Dropping Out?

Driver license applicants less than 18 years old must have a Driving Eligibility Certificate, high school diploma or its equivalent to be eligible for a North Carolina driving permit or license. The Driving Eligibility Certificate must be signed by the applicant's school administrator who certifies that the applicant is currently enrolled in school and making progress toward a high school diploma; or that substantial hardship would be placed on the applicant or the applicant's family if he or she does not receive a driver license. The steps in graduated licensing must still be followed even if the Driving Eligibility Certificate is issued due to hardship conditions. North Carolina does not issue a hardship driving permit or license.

DMV must revoke the driver license of any person under age 18 when it receives notice from the proper school authority that the person is no longer eligible for a Driving Eligibility Certificate. This revocation remains in effect until the person's 18th birthday unless a Driving Eligibility Certificate, high school diploma or GED Certificate is obtained.

Lose Control/Lose Your License

A loss of license will occur if a student receives a suspension for more than 10 consecutive days or receives an assignment to an alternative educational setting due to disciplinary action for more than 10 consecutive days. This suspension remains in effect for 12 months or until a Driving Eligibility Certificate is obtained.

Restrictions

For safety reasons, a driver license may be limited or restricted. Examples:

• A driver may only be permitted to operate a motor vehicle while wearing corrective lenses.

• A driver who passes the license examination may be issued a driver license restricted to using equipment necessary to safely operate the motor vehicle.

If your license is restricted, you must only drive within the limits of the restriction; otherwise you are considered to be driving without a license.

Required Documents

The Division of Motor Vehicles may copy the documents presented or hold the documents for a brief period of time to verify authenticity. Any document reflecting alteration will not be accepted.

Requirements are based on North Carolina General Statutes 20-7 and 20-11 and 6 CFR Part 37 of the Federal Register.

If you are applying for a driver license, a learner's permit or an ID card for the first time in North Carolina, you will need to provide proof of your full name and date of birth, your NC residence address, proof of your social security number (SSN) or documentation indicating your legal presence in the U.S. You will need to provide proof of vehicle liability insurance when applying for a driver license.

A North Carolina driver license, learner's permit or ID card that includes the notation "Not for Federal Identification" is a valid state-issued driver license, learner's permit, or ID card.

Beginning Oct. 1, 2020, a driver license, learner's permit or ID Card with "Not for Federal Identification" means you will need to provide additional documentation to fly on a commercial airline and enter any federal facility, military base and nuclear power plant that requires identification. You much contact the facility that you are visiting to determine what additional identification is required.

Applicants under Age 18 Applying for a Driver License or Learner's Permit:

If you are under age 18, you must provide either a Driving Eligibility Certificate, proof of graduation from high school, or submit a GED. You must also provide proof of completion of a driver education course which consists of 30 hours of classroom instruction and 6 hours behind wheel instruction.

	DOCUMENT	DETAILS
	Table (1) – PROOF OF IDENTITY AND DATE OF BIRTH REQUIREMENTS: You must provide proof of your identity and date of birth from the list of documents below.	
1.	Valid, unexpired United States passport	
2.	Certified copy of a birth certificate filed with a State Office of Vital Statistics or equivalent agency in the individual's state of birth	• Certified copy • No photocopies unless certified by Issuing agency
3.	Consular Report of Birth Abroad (CRBA) issued by the United States Department of State	• Form FS-240, DS-1350, or FS-545
4.	Valid, unexpired Permanent Resident Card issued by DHS or USCIS	• Form I-551
5.	Unexpired employment authorization document (EAD) issued by DHS	• Form I-766 or Form I-668B
6.	Unexpired foreign passport with a valid, unexpired U.S. visa affixed accompanied by the approved I-94 form documenting the applicant's most recent admittance into the United States.	
7.	Certificate of Naturalization issued by DHS	• Form N-550 or Form N-570
8.	Certificate of Citizenship issued by DHS	• Form N-560 or Form N-561
9.	REAL ID driver license or identification card showing full name	
10.	Driver License or State-issued Identification Card from North Carolina or another State, Puerto Rico, United States territory, or a Canadian Province	• Card received will be noted "Not for Federal Identification" • A driver license, learner's permit or ID card must be valid or expired less than 2 years
11.	Motor Vehicle Driver Record	• Card received will be noted "Not for Federal Identification" • Certified NC Motor Vehicle Record • Non-Certified NC Motor Vehicle Record • Certified Out-of-State Motor Vehicle Record

	DOCUMENT	DETAILS
12.	NC school transcript/registration signed by a school official, or diploma or GED from an NC school, community college or NC university	• Card received will be noted "Not for Federal Identification" • Driver Education Certificates, Driver Eligibility Certificates and report cards are not accepted as proof of identification.
13.	Valid unexpired US military ID, including DD-2, DD-214, OR US military Dependents Card, US Veteran Universal Access Card	• Card received will be noted "Not for Federal Identification" • Other than DD-214, documents submitted as a form of identification • must be valid and unexpired
14.	Certified document from a Register of Deeds or government agency in the US, Puerto Rico, US territories or Canada	• Card received will be noted "Not for Federal Identification" • Marriage certificate, divorce decree, court documents of name change
15.	Limited Driving Privilege issued by a NC court	• Card received will be noted "Not for Federal Identification" • Cannot be expired for more than 1 year
16.	Valid, unexpired documents issued by DHS/USCIS	• Card received will be noted "Not for Federal Identification" • Unexpired immigration document may be valid if accompanied by a letter from USCIS extending the expiration date (e.g. I-797)
17.	Court documents from US jurisdiction, Puerto Rico, US territories or Canada	• Card received will be noted "Not for Federal Identification" • Divorce Decree • Court order for name or gender change • Adoption Papers
Table (2) – SOCIAL SECURITY NUMBER REQUIREMENT: To obtain a driver license, learner's permit, or ID card, you must provide a Social Security Number (SSN). If you are not eligible for a SSN, you must provide document(s) indicating your legal presence in the United States.		
	DOCUMENT	DETAILS
1.	Social Security Card	No photocopies
2.	W-2 form	
3.	SSA-1099 form	
4.	Non-SSA- 1099 form	

	DOCUMENT	DETAILS
5.	Pay stub with the applicant's name and SSN	
6.	DD-214 with full social security number	Card received will be noted "Not for Federal Identification"
7.	Social security document reflecting full social security number	Card received will be noted "Not for Federal Identification"
8.	Military Record relecting the SSN with full social security number.	Card received will be noted "Not for Federal Identification"
9.	Medicaid or Medicare Card reflecting the SSN with full social security number	Card received will be noted "Not for Federal Identification"

Table (3) – PROOF OF RESIDENCY REQUIREMENTS- FOR ADULTS 18 OR OVER: Customers must show two documents reflecting their permanent North Carolina address.

	DOCUMENT	DETAILS
1.	Document issued by an agency of the United States or by the government of another nation	
2.	Document issued by another state	
3.	Document issued by the State of North Carolina, or a political subdivision of this State. This includes an agency or instrumentality of this state.	
4.	Preprinted bank or other corporate statement	
5.	Preprinted business letterhead	
6.	Pay stub with payee's address	
7.	Utility bill showing the address of the applicant	
8.	Contract for an apartment, house, modular unit, or manufactured home with a North Carolina address signed by the applicant	
9.	Receipt for personal property taxes paid	
10.	Receipt for real property taxes paid to a North Carolina locality	
11.	Current automobile insurance policy issued to the applicant and showing the applicant's address	

	DOCUMENT	DETAILS
12.	Monthly or quarterly financial statement	
13.	NC Vehicle Registration Card or title	
14.	NC Voter Precinct Card	
15.	NC School Records	

Table (4) – PROOF OF RESIDENCY REQUIREMENTS- FOR MINOR UNDER AGE OF 18: Minor customers must show two documents reflecting their permanent North Carolina address.

	DOCUMENT	DETAILS
1.	Correspondence from organizations (boy scout/girl scout, recreational teams, etc.)	
2.	N.C. School records	• Must present a letter from physician
3.	Magazine subscriptions	• No additional documentation needed
4.	Lease or housing contract showing minor as occupant	
5.	Tax records/returns reflecting minor as a dependent	
6.	Medical/hospitalization records	
7.	Hunting/fishing license	
8.	Social Security Card stub showing address	
9.	Preprinted bank statement or financial records	
10.	Preprinted business letter	
11.	Letter from homeless shelter	• Must present letter from the shelter in which you reside

Table (5) – PROOF OF LEGAL PRESENCE REQUIREMENTS: To obtain a driver license, learner permit or an identification card, you will need to show proof of legal presence in the United States. Based on your legal presence status, you may be required to present multiple documents.

	DOCUMENT	DETAILS
1.	Permanent Resident Card (Form I-551)	

	DOCUMENT	DETAILS
2.	Machine-Readable Immigrant Visa (MRIV) with Temp I-551 Language)	
3.	Temporary I-551 Stamp on Passport or I-94	
4.	Employment Authorization Card (Form I-766)	
5.	I-20 (F1, F2, M1, M2) Certification with I-94 Arrival/ Departure Document or Unexpired Foreign Passport with CBP Admission Stamp	
6.	DS2019 (J1, J2) Certification with I-94 Arrival/Departure Document or Unexpired Foreign Passport with CBP Admission Stamp	
7.	I-94 Arrival/Departure Records-Electronic I-94	
8.	Waiver Traveler/Waiver Business (WT/WB) Admission Stamp	
9.	U.S. Passport or U.S. Passport Card	
10.	Other Documents (Non-Student) w/Alien Number	Card received will be noted "Not for Federal Identification"
11.	I-220 B Order of Supervision w/I-766 card	Card received will be noted "Not for Federal Identification"
12.	I-512L Authorization for Parole of an Alien into the U.S. w/ supporting immigration documents (I-551, I-766 or I-94)	Card received will be noted "Not for Federal Identification"
13.	Unexpired Foreign Passport w/CBP Admission Stamp	Card received will be noted "Not for Federal Identification"

Table (6) – DEFERRED ACTION FOR CHILDHOOD ARRIVALS (DACA): To obtain a driver license, learner permit or an identification card, you will need to show proof of legal presence in the United States. Based on your legal presence status, you may be required to present multiple documents.

	DOCUMENT	DETAILS
1.	Employment Authorization Document reflecting Category C33	
2.	1-797 Notice of Action (Case type I-821) Approval Notice with valid "to and from" dates	Card received will be noted "Not for Federal Identification"

Table (7) – PROOF OF INSURANCE FOR DRIVER LICENSE: If you are obtaining a driver license, you will need to provide proof of liability insurance coverage from a North Carolina-licensed insurance carrier. The proof of insurance must reflect your name.

	DOCUMENT	DETAILS
1.	Form DL-123 from your insurance agent	
2.	Vehicle insurance policy reflecting your name and expiration dates	
3.	An insurance binder	
4.	An insurance card with your name, the policy number and issue and expiration dates	

Table (8) – NO FEE IDs: To obtain an identification card at no charge, you must also include one of the following items with your documents from tables 1-5.

	DOCUMENT	DETAILS
1.	Homeless	Must present letter from the shelter in which you reside
2.	Legally Blind	Must present a letter from physician
3.	70 years of age or older	No additional documentation needed
4.	Voter ID	
5.	Medically Cancelled	Your NC Driving Record must reflect that your driving status is medically cancelled
6.	Developmental Disability	Must present a letter from primary care provider

Liability Insurance Requirement

The N.C. General Assembly has enacted legislation to require some (but not all) driver license applicants in North Carolina to submit proof of automobile liability insurance coverage in order to obtain a North Carolina driver license.

Proof of liability insurance coverage applies to those:

- Applying for an original license, including transfers from out of state;
- Whose licenses are being restored after revocation or suspension; or
- Awarded a Limited Driving Privilege by the court.

Form DL-123, binders and certificates are valid only for 30 days from the date of issuance. This does not apply to applicants who do not own currently registered motor vehicles and who do not operate non-fleet private passenger motor vehicles that are owned by other persons. In such cases it is required that a certification of exemption (DL-123A) be signed at the driver license office.

> If you must show proof of financial responsibility, and to avoid inconveniences at the driver license office, obtain Form DL-123 from your insurance agent in advance of your visit.

The exemption restricts the driver to the operation of "Fleet Vehicles Only". To remove the restriction, the driver must pay a $13 duplicate fee and present proof of financial responsibility.

North Carolina's REAL ID

The REAL ID Act of 2005, mandated increased security standards for state-issued driver licenses and identification cards. In cooperation with the Department of Homeland Security, the North Carolina REAL ID is a single form of identification with increased security measures that meet the federal identification requirements for the Transportation Security Administration and federal facilities. A REAL ID is a driver license, learner permit or identification card with a gold star.

The REAL ID Act will directly impact travelers on domestic commercial airlines including unaccompanied minors (under the age of 18), visitors to federal facilities where identification is required including military installations, correctional facilities and nuclear power plants.

Residents that do not have a REAL ID can still access these federal facilities, but will be required to present additional documentation before access is granted. It is recommended that customers contact the federal agency (TSA and others) prior to visiting to inquire about the additional documentation needed for access. As required by federal law, non-REAL ID licenses and identification cards will display "NOT FOR FEDERAL IDENTIFICATION" on the face of the card.

The NCDMV began issuing REAL ID and "Not for Federal Identification" driver licenses, learner permits and identification cards in May 2017. All current fees for new issuances, renewals and duplicates are the same. There is no additional cost for a North Carolina REAL ID. Those wishing to obtain a REAL ID must visit a local NCDMV Driver License Office. Residents can call (919) 715-7000 to schedule an appointment.

Residents must first meet all necessary requirements for a driver license, permit, or identification card before being eligible to obtain a REAL ID issuance.

To obtain a REAL ID, the following required documents must be presented:

- Identity, Date of Birth and Legal Presence/Lawful Status**—one document containing the full name and date of birth
- Proof of Social Security Number—one document containing name and full Social Security Number
- Proof of Address—two documents showing name and permanent residence
- In the event of a name change, or changes in personal identifying information, official certified documentation must be provided reflecting the change.

Please visit *NCREALID.gov* to get a complete list of the required documents.

IMPORTANT: *All REAL IDs have a gold star. All non-REAL IDs will display "NOT FOR FEDERAL IDENTIFICATION" as required by federal law.*

Moving to North Carolina

A new resident has 60 days after establishing residence to obtain a North Carolina license or learner permit. If you hold a commercial driver license from another jurisdiction and wish to maintain a commercial license, you must apply for and receive a North Carolina commercial license within 30 days after becoming a resident.

DMV shall not issue a driver license or identification card to an applicant who has resided in this state for less than 12 months until the division has completed a search of the National Sex Offender Public Registry (North Carolina General Statute 20-9(i)).

A new resident applying for a Class C License may be required to be tested on the following:

• Knowledge test;

• Vision test;

• Traffic signs recognition test; and

• Driving skills test (if the examiner deems necessary).

A nonresident is, "Any person whose legal residence is in a state, territory, or jurisdiction other than North Carolina or in a foreign country."

Examples of nonresidents:

• Salesmen whose homes are in other states who travel through North Carolina;

• Out-of-state college students who intend to return to their home states upon completion of their education in North Carolina;

• Members of the armed forces stationed in North Carolina who intend to return to their home states; and

• Spouses of nonresident members of the armed forces stationed in North Carolina.

North Carolina's Driver License and Identification Card

Digital imaging is used to obtain and store customer photos and signatures. The driver license/identification card is equipped with a bar code system that houses customer data.

North Carolina issues driver licenses, learner permits and ID cards from a central location. Customers who take required tests and have their photos made at the local driver license office will receive a temporary driving certificate valid for 60 days. Customers may keep their current license or ID card to use as a photo ID until their new license is delivered by mail within 60 days.

Driver licenses may be renewed up to six months before a customer's birthday. Customers are encouraged to renew their license as early as possible to make sure their new license arrives on time. Visit *MyNCDMV.gov* for more information.

DMV issues a vertical license/ID card to applicants under the age of 21. As added protection, applicants under age 18 receive license/ID cards with two color bars, red and yellow, next to their photo indicating their 18th and 21st birthdays. Applicants under age 21 receive one red color bar indicating the date they reach the age of 21.

Renewal and Duplicate Licenses

Renewal

The DMV will mail you a reminder card about 60 days before expiration of your license listing the number of years it will be valid. You may be eligible for online renewal (see page 4). If you must visit a Driver License office for your renewal, the vision and traffic sign tests are required. It is not necessary to have the reminder card in order to renew your driver license. A driver license may be renewed anytime within 180 days prior to expiration. If you do not have your current or expired license at renewal, you will be required to show the examiner two documents of identification as outlined.

Renewal By Mail (Temporary License)

A resident of North Carolina who has been residing outside the state for at least 30 continuous days may also renew their license by mail. This is a temporary license which expires 60 days after the person returns to North Carolina or on the expiration date shown on the face of the license, whichever comes first. The following requirements must be met:

• Must have a permanent North Carolina verifiable residence address.

• Must have a North Carolina Class C driver license that has not expired for more than two years

• Must have a photo on file with DMV that was issued within the last five years

• NCDMV must have a record of your Social Security number or a document issued by the United States government indicating legal presence.

• A vision statement form signed by a licensed physician must be provided.

• A signed and dated National Sex Offender Affidavit is required and will be provided.

• Customer must not be older than 72 on the date of request to renew by mail

• The customer may renew by mail every other renewal cycle.

A commercial or a full provisional license cannot be renewed by mail.

Military

A resident of North Carolina who is active duty Military residing outside the state may also request a driver license renewal by mail. The following requirements must be met:

• Must have a permanent North Carolina verifiable residence address or, if you do not have a permanent North Carolina verifiable residence address, you may provide the address of a verifiable North Carolina host family

• Must provide military orders and a copy of military identification card, both front and back

- Driver license renewal may be made for more than one year prior to expiration date when accompanied by military papers showing active duty status
- Must have a North Carolina Class C driver license that has not expired by more than two years
- Must have a photo on file with DMV that was issued within the last eight years
- NCDMV must have a record of your Social Security number or a document issued by the United States government indicating legal presence
- A vision statement form is required and must be provided. A vision waiver can be submitted for active duty military currently in a war zone (documentation required)
- A signed and dated National Sex Offender Affidavit is required and will be provided
- Customer must not be older than 72 on the date of request to renew by mail
- A driver license with a military designation may be renewed no more than two times during the license holder's lifetime.
- Military spouse and dependents may also renew by mail.
- A dependent holding a full provisional driver license can upgrade to a Class C driver license if their license has not been expired for more than one year and they are 18 years of age. The customer will need to meet the issuance requirements and complete the application.

A military customer does not need to go to a driver license office when they return to North Carolina. They will not need to go in until time to renew their license. Example: If the military customer returns to North Carolina in 2010 and his license does not expire until 2014, the customer will not need to go into an office for renewal until 2014.

Veterans

Qualified North Carolina military veterans are able to carry the designation "VETERAN" on their driver licenses and identification cards.

Military veterans requested the designation to assist them in obtaining military discounts from a wide variety of retailers and service providers without having to show their military discharge form. Putting the designation on the driver license or ID card will enable the state's veterans to show their photo ID and their veteran status at the same time. Many states are making such designations available.

Veterans who are interested in applying for the designation should take their DD-214 discharge form to their local driver license office to show they have been honorably discharged. They can request the designation be added to their license at their next renewal at no additional charge.

The Division accepts the following documents as proof of a veteran's Honorable Discharge status:

US Military ID – Valid unexpired U.S. military ID, including DD-2, DD-214, or U.S Military Dependents Card, U.S. Veteran Universal Access Card.

DD-214 – Certificate of Release or Discharge

DD-215 – Certificate of Release or Discharge

WD AGO 53/55 – Report of Separation

NAVMC 78-PD – Notice of Separation

NAVPERS – Separation of Service

If a veteran would like to add the designation at any other time, they may present the discharge form and request a duplicate license for the usual fee at any driver license office.

Duration and Renewal of License

Your license will expire on your birthday depending upon your age at time of issuance as shown below:

Age at Time of Issuance	Duration
18–65	8 years
66 and older	5 years

* In no event shall a license expire later than the authorization for the applicant's legal presence in the United States.

Duplicate

If your license is not expired, suspended or cancelled, visit the nearest driver license office and provide your driver license to apply for a duplicate. To replace a lost or stolen license, you may show the examiner two documents of identification approved by the DMV. *This type of transaction may also be completed online. (See page 4.)*

Address Changes

If your address changes from the address on your driver license, you must notify the division of the change within 60 days and obtain a duplicate license. If you do not move, but your address changes due to a governmental action, you are not in violation of this law. *This type of transaction may also be completed online. (See page 4.)*

Name Changes

A person whose name changes from the name stated on a driver license must notify the division of the change within 60 days after the change occurs and obtain a duplicate driver license stating the new name. The Division of Motor Vehicles confirms your name with the Social Security Online Verification System; please visit your local Social Security Administration Office at least 24 hours before changing your name with DMV. Name changes can be completed with:

• A certified marriage certificate issued by a governmental agency;

- Documented proof from the courts or the Register of Deeds establishing that the name change was officially accomplished; or
- Execution of a notarized DL-101 (obtain this document from a DMV office)

All documentation must be provided by the appropriate government agency of the United States, Puerto Rico, U.S. territories or Canada.

Identification Cards

Any resident of North Carolina can be issued a special identification card. You will need the same documents as required for a driver license: proof of identity and residency, as well as the Social Security requirements. The fee for a special identification card is $13. This fee is exempt for residents who are legally blind, at least 70 years old, homeless or whose license has been cancelled for certain medical reasons.

Schedule of Fees (subject to change)

Type of Fee	Regular	CDL
Driver License		
Application Fee	N/A	$40
Class A	$5/yr.*	$20/yr.*
Class B	$5/yr.*	$20/yr.*
Class C	$5/yr.*	$20/yr.*
Motorcycle Endorsement (with regular issuance)	$2.30/yr.*	$2.30/yr.*
CDL Endorsements	N/A	$4/yr.*
Duplicate License	$13	$13
Permits and Other Fees		
Learner Permit	$20	$20
Motorcycle Learner Permit	$20	N/A
Duplicate	$13	$13
Special Identification Card	$13	
Restoration Fee	$65	
Driving Clinic Fee	$65	
Service Fee	$50	
DWI Restoration Fee	$130	
Graduated Licensing		
Limited Learner Permit (Level 1)	$20	N/A
Limited Provisional License (Level 2)	$20	N/A
Full Provisional License (Level 3)	$5 yr.*	N/A
Temporary Permit	$15	N/A
Duplicate	$13	N/A

NOTE: *Fees are calculated on annual basis.*

Other Services

Voter Registration

You may register to vote or make changes to your current voter registration when applying for a North Carolina driver license, learner permit or an identification card.

Organ Donor Program

If you wish to be an organ donor, you may indicate your decision when you apply for or renew your North Carolina driver license or ID card. Donors' driver licenses and ID cards carry a heart symbol on the front of their cards, representing their consent to be an organ and eye donor. It is highly recommended that you discuss your wishes with your family and make sure they are aware of your decision. For more information, visit *www.DonateLifeNC.org*.

Selective Service System Registration

DMV is required to notify any male U.S. citizen or immigrant between the ages of 18 and 25 who is applying for a driver license, commercial driver license or ID card that his application for the license or ID card serves as his consent to be registered with the Selective Service System (in compliance with the Military Selective Service Act, 50 U.S.C. 3801 et seq.

Requirements for Sex Offender Registration Program

DMV must provide notice to each person applying for a driver license, learner's permit or identification card that, if the person is a sex offender, the person is required by law to register with the sheriff's office in their county of residence. DMV obtains reports from the National Sex Offender Public Registry. (North Carolina General Statutes 20-9(i) and 20-37.7)

- If the person is a current registered sex offender in another state, DMV will not issue a license, permit or ID card until the person submits proof of registration with the sheriff's office.

- If the person is not registered in another state, DMV must require the person to sign an affidavit and may issue the card applied for.

- If the national sex offender database is unavailable, DMV must require the person to sign an affidavit and may issue the card applied for.

- If the Division accesses the National Sex Offender Public Registry and verifies that the person is currently registered as a sex offender in North Carolina or any other state, the Division shall not issue a Commercial Driver License with a Passenger (P) or School Bus (S) endorsement.

Chapter 2
Alcohol and the Law

Everyone's driving is impaired at a blood alcohol concentration, or BAC, of 0.08 percent, but many people are affected at much lower levels. Research shows that the risk of being involved in a crash increases when the alcohol level is 0.05 percent, and at 0.08 percent, the risk of causing a fatal crash is even greater.

Driving While Impaired

In 1983, the North Carolina General Assembly enacted the Safe Roads Act. This act repealed all previous laws on drunk driving in North Carolina and replaced them with a single offense of "Driving While Impaired–DWI."

If an officer charges you with driving while impaired, you will be asked to take a chemical test of your breath or blood. Refusal to perform any required test will result in the immediate revocation of your driver license for at least 30 days and an additional, minimum 12-month revocation by the DMV. In certain instances, after six months of the willful refusal revocation has elapsed, the judge may issue a limited driving privilege.

If your blood alcohol concentration test shows a BAC of 0.08 percent or more (0.04 or more, if you are driving a commercial motor vehicle), your driving privilege will be revoked immediately for a minimum of 30 days. Additionally, the results of your chemical test or the fact that you refused to take the test will be admissible as evidence in court.

Driving while impaired can be proven in one of two ways:

- By proving the driver's physical or mental fitness are appreciably impaired by alcohol, drugs or a combination of both; or

- By proving the driver's blood alcohol concentration is 0.08 percent or more, or 0.04 or more, if you are driving a Commercial Motor Vehicle.

DWI Laws:

- Allow enforcement agencies to set up road blocks to check for impaired drivers;

- Prohibit drivers from consuming any alcoholic beverage, including beer, while driving;

- Prohibit the transport of an open container of any alcoholic beverage, including in the passenger area of the car;

- Prohibit the possession of alcoholic beverages (open or closed) in the passenger area of a commercial motor vehicle while upon any highway, street or public vehicular area;

- Provide for different levels of severity of punishment based on the severity of the offense;

- Require persons who are convicted of DWI for the second time to serve a jail sentence;

- Attempt to punish DWI offenders, but also try to help them deal with problems they may have with alcohol;

- Require that repeat DWI offenders or persons with high BACs be checked to see if they have an alcohol problem;
- Require persons with lower BACs to attend alcohol safety schools; and
- Require anyone convicted of DWI to obtain a substance abuse assessment prior to the reinstatement of driving privileges.

> If you are convicted of DWI while your license is revoked for an earlier DWI conviction, the court may order your vehicle seized and sold.

If you are convicted of DWI:

First conviction: Mandatory revocation of your driver license for a period of one year.

Second conviction: Mandatory driver license revocation for a period of four years when convicted of a prior offense which occurred within three years of the current offense for which the license is being revoked.

Third conviction: Mandatory, permanent driver license revocation if at least one of the prior convictions occurred within the past five years.

Fourth conviction: Mandatory permanent driver license revocation. The fourth conviction is considered a felony if the three prior DWI convictions occurred within the past seven years.

Blood Alcohol Concentration Restrictions

A blood alcohol concentration restriction will be required when a license is restored following a suspension for DWI or when a Limited Driving Privilege is issued following a DWI conviction.

On the first restoration, the alcohol concentration restriction will be 0.04. On a second or subsequent restoration, the alcohol concentration restriction will be 0.00. Additionally, if you are convicted of DWI in a commercial motor vehicle, driving after consuming alcohol or drugs while under the age of 21 or felony death by vehicle, the alcohol concentration restriction will be 0.00.

Furthermore, a conviction of Driving While Impaired with a BAC of 0.15 or more, or another conviction within the past seven years, will require an ignition interlock device to be installed on the vehicle.

Alcohol and the Young Driver

The legal age to purchase any alcoholic beverage in North Carolina is 21. It is against the law for any person who is younger than 21 years of age to purchase or to attempt to purchase alcohol.

The law requires a one-year driver license revocation upon conviction for:

- Any underage person who attempts to purchase or purchases an alcoholic beverage;
- Any underage person who aids or abets another who attempts to purchase or purchases an alcoholic beverage;

- Any underage person who obtains or attempts to obtain alcoholic beverages by using or attempting to use a fraudulent driver license or other ID or another person's driver license or ID; or

- Any person who permits his or her driver license or any other ID to be used by an underage person to purchase or attempt to purchase an alcoholic beverage.

- Any person who gives an alcoholic beverage to any underage person.

> If a driver who is less than 21 years old is convicted for an offense of driving with any amount of alcohol or drugs in his/her body, his/her license will be revoked for one year.

*DWI laws are subject to change pending legislation. For updates on laws that may impact this section, visit **www.ncleg.net**.*

Chapter 3
Your Driving Privilege

Points

Driver License Points

If you are convicted of certain motor vehicle violations in North Carolina, driver license points are placed against your driving record. If you accumulate seven points, you may be assigned to a driver improvement clinic. The clinic fee is $65. Upon satisfactory completion of the clinic, three points are deducted from your driving record. If you accumulate as many as 12 points within a three-year period, your license may be suspended. The accumulation of eight points within three years following the reinstatement of your license can result in a second suspension.

If your driver license is suspended by the point system, it may be taken for:

- 60 days for the first suspension;
- 6 months for the second; and
- 12 months for the third.

When your driving privilege is reinstated, all previous driver license points are canceled. This does not pertain to insurance points.

Points are given for the following offenses:

Conviction	Point Value
Passing a stopped school bus	5
Aggressive driving	5
Reckless driving	4
Hit and run, property damage only	4
Following too closely	4
Driving on wrong side of road	4
Illegal passing	4
Failure to yield right of way to pedestrian pursuant to G.S. 20-158 (b) (2) b.	4
Failure to yield right of way to bicycle, motor scooter or motorcycle	4
Running through stop sign	3
Speeding in excess of 55 mph	3
Failure to yield right of way	3
Running through red light	3
No driver license or license expired more than one year	3
Failure to stop for siren	3
Driving through safety zone	3

No liability insurance	3
Failure to report accident where such report is required	3
Speeding in a school zone in excess of the posted school zone speed limit	3
Failure to properly restrain a child in a restraint or seat belt	2
All other moving violations	2
Littering pursuant to G.S. 14-399 when the littering involves the use of a motor vehicle	1

Schedule of point values for conviction of violations while operating a commercial motor vehicle:

Conviction	*Point Value*
Passing stopped school bus	8
Rail-highway crossing violation	6
Careless and reckless driving in violation of G.S.20-140(f)	6
Speeding in violation of G.S. 20-141(j3)	6
Aggressive driving	6
Reckless driving	5
Hit and run, property damage only	5
Following too closely	5
Driving on wrong side of road	5
Illegal passing	5
Failure to yield right of way to pedestrian pursuant to G.S. 20-158 (b) (2) b.	5
Failure to yield right of way to bicycle, motor scooter or motorcycle	5
Running through stop sign	4
Speeding in excess of 55 miles per hour	4
Failure to yield right of way	4
Running through red light	4
No driver license or license expired more than one year	4
Failure to stop for siren	4
Driving through safety zone	4
No liability insurance	4
Failure to report accident where such report is required	4
Speeding in a school zone in excess of the posted school zone speed limit	4
Possessing alcoholic beverage in the passenger area of a commercial motor vehicle	4
All other moving violations	3

Littering pursuant to G.S. 14-399 when the littering involves the use of a motor vehicle	1

No points shall be assessed for convictions of the following offenses:
- Overload;
- Overlength;
- Overwidth;
- Overheight;
- Illegal parking;
- Carrying concealed weapon;
- Improper plates;
- Improper registration;
- Improper muffler;
- Improper display of license plates or dealer's tags;
- Unlawful display of emblems and insignia
- Failure to display a current inspection certificate

Any person who commits an offense for which points may be assessed for violations while operating a commercial motor vehicle may be assessed double the amount of any fine or penalty authorized by statute.

Insurance Points
Insurance companies use a different point system to determine insurance rates. If you have any questions concerning insurance points, contact your insurance agent.

Suspensions
In addition to criminal penalties that the court might mandate, conviction of certain traffic offenses will result in the loss of your driving privilege.

Your driving privilege will be revoked for at least 30 days if you are convicted of:
- Driving any vehicle more than 15 miles per hour over the speed limit, if you are driving at a speed higher than 55 mph.

It will be taken for 60 days if you are convicted of:
- A second charge of speeding over 55 mph and more than 15 mph above the speed limit within one year; or
- Speeding plus reckless driving on the same occasion.

The DMV can also suspend your license for the following:
- Two convictions of speeding over 55 mph within a period of 12 months;
- One conviction of speeding over 55 mph and one conviction of reckless driving within a year;
- A conviction of willful racing with another motor vehicle, whether it is prearranged or unplanned;

- A suspended court sentence or part of a sentence mandating that you must not operate a motor vehicle for a specified period of time; and/or
- A conviction for speeding over 75 mph, in certain cases

In cases like the above, the DMV may suspend your driving privilege as soon as it receives the conviction report from the court. If your driving privilege is revoked, you may have the right to a hearing in the judicial district where you reside. To request a hearing, call at (919)715-7000 or click on Contact Us at MyNCDMV.gov. You will be notified by mail of the time and place for the hearing. At the hearing you may state any facts that you think should entitle you to driving privileges or to a reduction of the suspension period.

If you believe your driving privilege should not have been revoked and the hearing gives you no help, you may appeal the DMV's decision within 30 days to the Superior Court of the county where you live. The court will review your case to see if there were proper grounds for revoking your driving privilege.

Offense	*Suspension Time*
Manslaughter	1 year
Death by vehicle	1 year
Manslaughter while under the influence of an impairing substance	Permanent
Assault with a motor vehicle	1 year
Failure to stop and give aid when involved in an accident	1 year
Speeding in excess of 55 mph and at least 15 mph over the legal limit while attempting to avoid arrest	1 year
Prearranged racing with another motor vehicle on the highway	*3 years
Watching, betting on or loaning a car for prearranged racing	*3 years
Willful refusal to submit to a blood or breath alcohol test	1 year
Two charges of reckless driving committed within 12 months	1 year
Attempting to obtain a license or learner permit under false pretense	1 year
Failure to yield right of way when entering an intersection, turning at a stop or yield sign, entering a roadway, upon the approach of an emergency vehicle or at a highway construction or maintenance area when the offense results in serious bodily injury	90 days and $500

When an officer finds that someone has loaned or is operating a motor vehicle willfully in prearranged racing, he/she will seize the vehicle. If the person is convicted, the court may order the vehicle sold at public auction.
NOTE: *If the court makes a finding that a longer period of revocation is appropriate, the division must revoke for two years.*

Out-of-State Conviction

Convictions occurring outside North Carolina may result in your license being suspended or revoked just as if the violations occurred in this state. If a suspension occurs, the Division must notify you by correspondence of the effective date of the suspension.

Failure to Appear and/or to Pay a Fine

When the division receives notification that you failed to appear in court or pay court fines for a citation received in North Carolina or another state, you will be notified of the effective date of the revocation if not paid prior to the date indicated on the correspondence. The revocation will remain in effect until the division is notified by the court that the citation or fine has been complied with and may result in you having to pay appropriate fees to DMV to obtain a duplicate license. Complying with the citation does not relieve you of the consequences for the actual offense if convicted.

Provisional Licensee (under age 18)

There are other rules that apply to persons under 18 years of age. If you are a provisional licensee, your license may be suspended for:

- 30 days, upon conviction of a second moving violation occurring within a 12-month period;
- 90 days, upon conviction of a third moving violation occurring within a 12-month period; and
- Six months, upon conviction of a fourth moving violation occurring within a 12-month period.

Some examples of moving violations:
- Passing a stopped school bus;
- Reckless driving;
- Hit-and-run;
- Following too closely;
- Driving on the wrong side of the road;
- Illegal passing;
- Running through a stop sign or red light;
- Failure to yield right of way;
- Failure to stop for an emergency siren; and
- Speeding.

Driver License Restoration

North Carolina law requires that a restoration fee of $65 be paid to the DMV before a suspension or revocation can be cleared. (This fee is not required if the license was taken for medical or health reasons following a medical evaluation.) A $130 restoration fee is required when the revocation results from a DWI conviction. Also, a service fee of $50 is required upon restoration of a revoked or suspended driver license unless the license was surrendered to the court or mailed to the DMV before the effective date of the suspension or revocation.

For the reinstatement of your driving privilege:

1. Visit any driver license office;
2. Provide proof of identity, i.e., driver license or two (2) other acceptable forms of i.d.;
3. Pay a restoration and/or service fee;
4. Reapply for a driver license;
5. Take required tests, if applicable;
6. Provide proof of insurance if required, and
7. Pay for new license issuance.

Chapter 4

Your Driving

Good driving skills should be developed and practiced at all times. You should also know your physical and mental limitations and not drive a vehicle when you are too tired or sleepy. When traveling long distances, plan ahead, know your route and be alert to the driving conditions. Your ability to safely operate a motor vehicle may save your life as well as the lives of others.

Driver Safety

Driver Condition

Your driving is affected by your physical and mental health. To obtain a driver license, you must be in good health. If you have health problems that are serious and long term in nature, they will likely come to the attention of the DMV. More often, health problems are short term, like suffering from colds, headaches or flu. You should remember that any time you are not feeling well, your driving is likely to be different. You may be less alert and less responsive than normal.

Drowsy Driving

According to the National Sleep Foundation (NSF), your number one responsibility is to get yourself and your passengers to your destination safely. When behind the wheel, you always need to be alert and focused on the job of driving. At 55 mph, a vehicle travels the length of a football field in 3.7 seconds. This is no time for a "mini" snooze. On the roads more traveled, being an attentive driver and looking out for the one who isn't, is increasingly important. Drive focused. Stay safe.

Drowsy driving causes thousands of crashes, injuries and deaths each year. Sadly, these numbers represent only the tip of the iceberg since drowsy driving is seriously under-reported, according to the NSF.

The NSF reports that crashes caused by drowsy driving are often serious and occur most often on high-speed rural highways when the driver is alone.

Drowsy driving could happen to anyone. Some warning signs include:
• You cannot remember the last few miles driven.

• You hit a rumble strip or drift from your lane.

• You yawn repeatedly.

• You have difficulty focusing or keeping your eyes open.

Tips to Prevent Drowsy Driving:
• Get a full night of rest before driving. If you become tired while driving, stop. A short nap (15 to 45 minutes) and consuming caffeine can help temporarily.

• Stop regularly when driving long distances. Get out of the car at least every 2 hours to stretch and walk briskly.

• Try to set a limit of 300-400 miles of driving per day.

- Avoid taking medications that cause drowsiness.
- If you are tired and in danger of falling asleep, you cannot predict when a "mini" sleep may occur. A driver cannot react to road dangers when tired. Getting enough sleep will not only help you feel better, it can save your life.

Distracted Driving

Distracted driving is any activity that could divert a person's attention away from the primary task of driving. All distractions endanger driver, passenger and bystander safety. These types of distractions include:

- Texting
- Using a cell phone
- Eating and drinking
- Talking to passengers
- Grooming
- Reading, including maps
- Using a navigation system
- Watching a video
- Adjusting a radio, CD player, or MP3 player

Distractions

No matter what the distraction, inattentive drivers exhibit similar behavior. Distractions cause drivers to react more slowly to traffic conditions or events, such as a car stopping to make a turn or pulling out from a side road. Inattentive drivers fail more often to recognize potential hazards such as pedestrians or debris in the road. Also, distractions make it more difficult to conduct preventive or evasive moves to avoid a crash because many distractions force a driver to take at least one hand off the steering wheel.

Cell Phones

Cell phones can be a lifesaver in an emergency; however, they also can be distracting. Below are North Carolina laws and reminders to help you avoid letting the cell phone become a deadly distraction:

- It is unlawful to use a cell phone for email or text messages while operating a vehicle on a public street or highway or public vehicular area;
- Drivers less than 18 years of age are not permitted to use a cell phone or any additional technology associated with a cell phone while operating a motor vehicle on a public street or highway or public vehicular area while the vehicle is in motion. Exceptions: calling 911 in an emergency;
- No person shall operate a school bus on a public street or highway or public vehicular area while using a cell phone or any other technology associated with a mobile device;
- Use your cell phone only if it is absolutely necessary and for the sole purpose of communicating regarding emergency situations or contacting parent, legal guardian or spouse;

- If you must use your phone, do so at a safe time and place;
- Ask a passenger in the car to place the call for you and, if possible, speak in your place;
- Do not feel like you must answer the phone when it rings. Let someone leave a message and you can return the call when you are stopped at a safe location;
- Secure your phone in the car so that it does not become a projectile in a crash.

Medications

Prescriptions and over-the-counter medications can affect your driving. Before you take any medication, find out how it will affect you. Try to do as little driving as possible while taking any type of medication. If you must drive, be especially careful. You may not be as alert as usual.

Alcohol

Alcohol reduces your ability to drive safely. No one drives as well after drinking alcohol, even though some people may look and act as though they are unaffected.

About 38 percent of all traffic fatalities involve alcohol.

Alcohol affects most areas of your brain, so the effects are wide-ranging and impossible to compensate. Alcohol is a depressant. This means alcohol:

- Slows brain functions so that you cannot respond to situations, make decisions or react quickly.
- Reduces your ability to judge how fast you are moving or your distance from other cars, people or objects.
- Gives you false confidence — you may take greater risks because you think your driving is better than it really is.
- Makes it harder to do more than one thing – while you concentrate on steering, you could miss seeing traffic lights, cars entering from side streets or pedestrians.
- Affects your sense of balance - very important if you ride a motorcycle.
- Makes you sleepy.

The only thing that sobers up a drinker is time. Coffee, a big meal or cold showers will not work.

Do not drink and drive.

- Plan ahead and arrange alternative transport.
- Share a taxi with friends.
- Use public transportation.
- Stay overnight at a friend's place.
- Ride with a driver who has not been drinking.
- Arrange for a friend or relative to give you a ride.

(Source: National Sleep Foundation & National Highway Traffic Safety Administration (NHTSA)

Protecting Yourself and Your Passengers

No one can be completely protected from being in a crash. You cannot predict what other drivers will do.

During an average lifetime of driving, we face about a one-in-three chance of being seriously injured or killed in a motor vehicle crash.

Seat Belts

The driver and all passengers in a motor vehicle manufactured with seat belts shall have a seat belt properly fastened about his or her body at all times when the vehicle is in forward motion on a street or highway in this state. Children under age 16 should be in an age and weight appropriate restraint. Under the seat belt law, all occupants MUST wear seat belts even if the vehicle is equipped with air bags. If the vehicle is equipped with automatic shoulder harnesses, the lap belt MUST also be worn.

Exemptions to the seat belt law:

- A driver or occupant of a noncommercial motor vehicle with a medical or physical condition that prevents appropriate restraint by a seat belt or with a professionally certified mental phobia against the wearing of vehicle restraints;

- A motor vehicle operated by a rural letter carrier of the United States Postal Service while performing duties as a rural letter carrier, and a motor vehicle operated by a newspaper delivery person while actually engaged in delivery of newspapers along the person's specified route;

- A driver or passenger frequently stopping and leaving the vehicle or delivering property from the vehicle if the speed of the vehicle between stops does not exceed 20 miles per hour;

- Any vehicle registered and licensed as a property-carrying vehicle while being used for agricultural purposes in intrastate commerce.

- A motor vehicle not required to be equipped with seat belts by law; and

- Any occupant of a motor home other than the driver and front seat passengers, provided the motor home has at least four of the following facilities: cooking, refrigeration or icebox, self-contained toilet, heating or air-conditioning, portable water supply system with a faucet and sink, separate 110-115-volt electrical power supply or an LP gas supply.

- Situations where all seating positions equipped with child passenger restraint systems or seat belts are occupied;

Child Safety

Each year hundreds of North Carolina children are seriously injured or killed in automobile crashes. In fact, the number one threat to the lives of young children is the automobile accident. Only crash-tested child safety seats can reduce these tragedies. Since small children cannot make safety choices for themselves, adults must make sure children are protected every time they ride in cars. Infants and small children must be placed in safety seats that are specially designed for them and have been crash-tested. Properly used safety seats could save seven out of every 10 children who are killed while unrestrained. Always read and follow the manufacturer's instructions for using the safety seat. The best seat for your child is a safety seat that is used every time the child rides in a car. It must fit in your car(s) and have a harness or shield system that is comfortable for the child. The seat should be one you are able and willing to use every time an infant or small child rides in your car. Safety seats are often available through low-cost rental programs operated by local service groups, hospitals and health departments.

Child Seats

Every driver transporting one or more passengers younger than 16 years of age must make sure that each passenger under age 16 is properly secured in a child passenger restraint system or a seat belt which meets the federal safety standards that were in effect at the time it was manufactured. A child under age 8 and weighing less than 80 pounds must be properly secured in a weight appropriate child passenger restraint system. If the vehicle is equipped with an active passenger-side front air bag and the vehicle has a rear seat, then a child under age 5 and weighing less than 40 pounds must be properly secured in the rear seat unless the child restraint system is designed for use with a front air bag system. If there are no available seating positions in the vehicle equipped with a lap and shoulder belt to properly secure the weight appropriate child restraint system, a child under age 8 and between 40 and 80 pounds can be restrained by a properly fitted lap belt only.

For information about child safety seats, contact:

University of North Carolina Highway Safety Research Center
Bolin Creek Center   Phone: 1-800-672-4527 (in NC only)
730 Martin Luther King Blvd.   or (919) 962-2202
Chapel Hill, NC 27514-5738

Booster Seats and Seat Belts for Children

Booster seats that meet federal motor vehicle safety standards should be used for children who have outgrown their standard safety seats until they are big enough for seat belts. Adult seat belts should not be used for children until they are big enough for the seat belt to fit correctly. The lap seat belt must fit snugly across the child's hips, not across the stomach. The shoulder portion of a lap/shoulder belt must fall across the shoulder and chest, not across the face or throat. For shoulder belts that do not fit, belt-positioning booster seats designed to raise a child up for a proper fit of the lap and shoulder belts are readily available.

Children and Air Bags

Air bags save lives. They work best when everyone is buckled and children are properly restrained in the back seat. Children riding in the front seat can be seriously injured or killed when an air bag comes out in a crash. An air bag is not a soft, billowy pillow. To do its important job, an air bag comes out of the dashboard at up to 200 miles per hour — faster than the blink of an eye.

The force of an air bag can hurt those who are too close to it. Drivers can help prevent air bag-related injuries to adults and children by following critical safety points.

Child Safety Points:
• Children age 12 and under should ride buckled up in a rear seat; and
• Infants in rear-facing child safety seats should NEVER ride in the front seat of a vehicle with a passenger-side air bag. Small children should ride in a rear seat in child safety seats approved for their age and size.

Adult Safety Points:
• Everyone should buckle-up with both lap and shoulder belts on every trip. Air bags are supplemental protection devices;

• The lap belt should be worn under the abdomen and low across the hips. The shoulder portion should come over the collarbone away from the neck and cross over the breastbone. The shoulder belt in most new cars can be adjusted on the side pillar to improve fit; and

• Driver and front passenger seats should be moved as far back as practical, particularly for shorter-statured people.

North Carolina Motorcycle Safety Helmet Law
All operators and passengers on motorcycles and mopeds must wear a motorcycle safety helmet of a type that complies with Federal Motor Vehicle Safety Standard (FMVSS) 218.

What to look for in a legal helmet:
• **A thick inner liner which includes a firm inner liner of polystyrene foam** that is about one inch thick. In some helmets this may be covered by a comfort liner, but you can feel the thickness. (Non-compliant helmets normally contain no liner or a thin soft foam padding.)

• **A DOT sticker which will show the symbol "DOT" permanently installed** by the manufacturer on the back of the helmet. (Some "novelty type" helmets are supplied with a separate "DOT" sticker or one can be purchased separately and placed on the helmet by the motorcyclist. This does not make this a compliant helmet.)

• **A manufacturer's label which is permanently attached in the interior of the helmet** by the manufacturer that includes the manufacturer's name or identification, precise model, size, month and year of manufacture, type of shell and liner construction materials and an instruction label for cleaning and care of the helmet.

Law on Transporting Children in the Back of a Pick-up Truck
North Carolina law prohibits children less than age 16 from riding in the open bed of a pick-up truck. *(NCGS §20-135.2B)* An open bed or open cargo area is a bed or cargo area without permanent overhead restraining construction.

The operator of the vehicle having an open bed or open cargo is responsible for compliance with this law. The statute does, however, contain some exemptions. The provisions for proper securement of children do not apply:

• If an adult is present in the bed or cargo area of the vehicle and is supervising the child;

• If the child is secured or restrained by a seat belt manufactured in compliance with Federal Motor Vehicle Safety Standard No. 208, installed to support a load strength of not less than 5,000 pounds for each belt, and of a type approved by the Commissioner;

• If an emergency situation exists;

• If the vehicle is being operated in a parade; or

• If the vehicle is being operated in an agricultural enterprise including providing transportation to and from the principal place of the enterprise.

Violators are issued tickets and are subject to a fine of $25. Violations of this law are defined as "infractions" and do not incur court costs, driver license points or insurance surcharges.

Weather Risk

It is dangerous and deadly to leave children and/or animals in a vehicle. During the spring and summer months, after sitting in the sun, with even a slightly opened window, the temperature can rise rapidly inside a parked vehicle. The temperature inside a vehicle can rise approximately 40-50 degrees higher than the outside temperature. Dehydration, heat stroke and death can result from overexposure to the heat. During winter months, snow can block a car's exhaust pipe, and warming up a car can cause carbon monoxide to back up into the car. Carbon monoxide is an invisible gas that has no smell, taste or color but is poisonous, even deadly.

General Driving

The Driver and Pedestrian

When you are driving, always yield right of way to pedestrians:

• At intersections without traffic signals, pedestrians have the right of way if they are in marked crosswalks or in unmarked crosswalks formed by imaginary lines extending from the sidewalks across the streets;

• At intersections controlled by ordinary traffic signals, pedestrians must obey the same signals as drivers traveling in the same direction. Pedestrians should not start to cross during a red or yellow signal;

• When crossing with a green signal, pedestrians have the right of way over all vehicles, including those turning across the paths of the pedestrians; and

• If a traffic signal changes to yellow or red while any pedestrian remains in the street, drivers must allow the pedestrian to complete the crossing safely.

• The law gives a blind pedestrian special consideration at an intersection where there are no traffic signals when the pedestrian extends a white cane, or a white cane with a red tip or has a guide dog.

At some intersections, special signals instruct pedestrians either to "Walk" or "Don't Walk". When these signals are operating, pedestrians must obey them rather than regular traffic signals.

- Pedestrians crossing with special pedestrian signals have the right of way just as they do while crossing with a green light.

- If you are moving through an intersection with a green signal and a pedestrian starts to cross in your path against the red signal, give a warning with your horn.

The law requires drivers to use the horn whenever a pedestrian may be affected by a turn, stop or start from a parked position. If the pedestrian does not stop, the driver must. Saving a pedestrian's life is always worth the driver's lost right of way. The safe driver yields right of way to a pedestrian whether the pedestrian is entitled to it or not.

Protecting Motorcyclists From Unsafe Movements

If a vehicle driver does not properly signal vehicle movements to a motorcycle operator and causes the motorcycle to change lanes or leave the roadway, the vehicle driver will be charged and fined as the law provides. If these actions result in a crash causing property damage or personal injury, the driver will be charged and fined as the law provides.

School Buses

The maximum speed limit for a school bus is 45 mph. School bus drivers travel more than half a million miles and transport almost three quarters of a million

children each school day. During the hours that school buses are operating (generally 7 – 9 a.m. and 2 – 4 p.m.), drivers should be especially careful. When a school bus displays its mechanical stop signal or flashing red lights to receive or discharge passengers, the driver of any other vehicle approaching the school bus must stop and not attempt to pass the school bus until the mechanical stop signal is withdrawn, the flashing red lights are turned off and the bus has started to move.

Children waiting for the bus or leaving the bus might dart out into traffic. Even when the school bus is not in sight, children at a bus stop sometimes will run into the street unexpectedly. **Always be careful around school buses and school bus stops.**

Below are specific rules for a variety of situations involving stopped school buses:

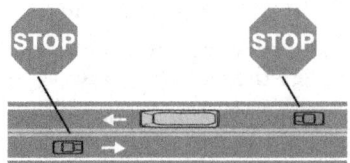

Two-lane roadway: When school bus stops for passengers, all traffic from both directions must stop.

Two-lane roadway with a center turning lane: When school bus stops for passengers, all traffic from both directions must stop.

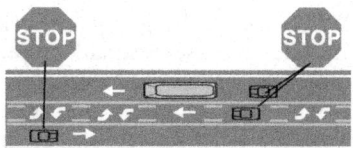

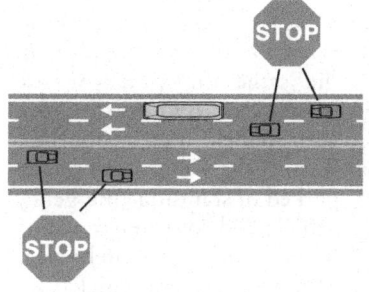

Four-lane roadway without a median separation: When school bus stops for passengers, all traffic from both directions must stop.

Divided highway of four lanes or more with a median separation: When school bus stops for passengers, only traffic following the bus must stop.

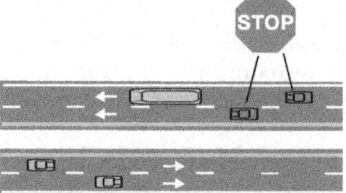

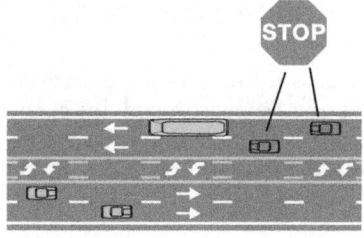

Roadway of four lanes or more with a center turning lane: When school bus stops for passengers, only traffic following the bus must stop.

Emergency and Law Enforcement Vehicles

Police cars, ambulances, fire engines and rescue vehicles with flashing lights and sirens always have the right of way.

Follow these guidelines when approaching or being approached by an emergency vehicle:

- As the emergency vehicle approaches (from ahead or behind), drive to the right-hand curb or edge of the road and stop completely;

- Remain stopped until the emergency vehicle has passed, or until directed to move by a traffic officer;

> All vehicles, regardless of direction of travel, must yield right of way to an approaching emergency vehicle. This does not apply to vehicles traveling in the opposite direction of the emergency vehicle(s) when traveling on a four-lane limited-access highway with a center median.

- Do not park within 100 feet of an emergency vehicle that has stopped to investigate an accident or to give assistance;

- Do not drive or park closer than one block from fire trucks responding to a fire alarm;

• Never drive a motor vehicle over a fire hose.

When approaching any authorized emergency vehicle (police, fire department, ambulance, rescue squad or public service vehicle that is being used to assist motorists or law enforcement officers with wrecked or disabled vehicles) that is parked or standing within 12 feet of the roadway with the emergency or warning lights activated, a driver is required to do the following:

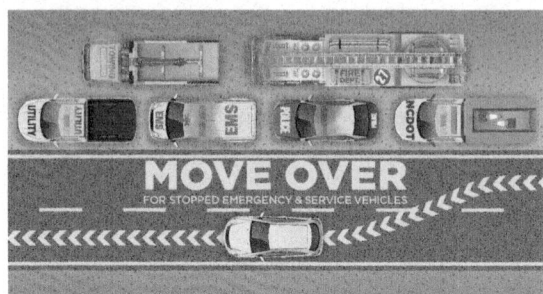

• On a highway with at least two lanes of traffic in the same direction you are traveling, you must move your vehicle into a lane that is not the lane nearest the parked or standing emergency vehicle and continue traveling in that lane until safely clear of the emergency vehicle.

• On a highway with only one lane of traffic in the same direction you are traveling, you must slow your speed and drive at a reduced, safe speed until completely past the emergency vehicle.

What Motorists Should Do When Stopped By Law Enforcement:

Law enforcement officers conduct traffic stops because they observe a traffic violation or are conducting a police investigation. Being stopped by a law enforcement officer can be a stressful experience but knowing what to do during the stop will help ensure your safety and the safety of others, including the officer.

The Driver

• When you see emergency lights and/or hear a siren behind you, stay calm, activate your turn signal, **pull the vehicle always to the right**, and off the travel portion of the highway at the nearest point where it is safe to do so.

• If there is not an obvious safe place to immediately stop the vehicle, turn on your emergency 4 way flashers and reduce your speed (by about 10 mph) to signal to the officer that you are aware of his or her presence. Continue driving and obey all traffic laws until you reach the nearest safe area to stop your vehicle.

• If an unmarked car is stopping you and you have a legitimate question or concern as to whether or not you are being stopped by an actual law enforcement officer, you may call 9-1-1 before pulling over. Report your name and location in order to verify that an actual law enforcement officer is conducting the traffic stop.

• After the vehicle stops, you should place the vehicle in "Park," roll down the window, turn off the engine, and silence any electronic devices and/or radio so that you can easily communicate with the officer. You and all passengers should **remain seated in the vehicle**. An officer may approach your vehicle on the driver or passenger side for safety reasons. **Do not** remove your seatbelt unless asked to do so by the officer.

- You should **place both hands on the steering wheel** and **instruct any passengers to keep their hands** in a position that is **clearly visible** to the officer at all times. Passengers in the back seat should place their hands on the back of the front seat. Keep your hands in plain view.

- If it is nighttime, the officer may direct a spotlight at your vehicle once stopped. To assist with visibility, turn on your interior lights as soon as you stop to help the officer see inside your vehicle.

- The officer will usually explain why he or she stopped you and may ask you questions. Under State law, you are required to identify yourself and provide your drivers license and registration for the vehicle. After establishing identification, you may choose whether or not to verbally respond to additional questions.

- If the officer is not in uniform he or she will show you his or her law enforcement credentials or you may ask to see them.

- If there is a firearm or other weapon in the vehicle, **do not** attempt to reach for the weapon. Under state law, any weapon should be in plain view or securely locked away, unless you or your passenger(s) have the proper permit. If you or your passenger(s) have a concealed weapon permit and a weapon is in the vehicle, you or your passenger(s) **must** inform the officer of that fact.

- **Do not exit the vehicle** or allow any passengers to exit the vehicle unless instructed to do so by the officer.

- If your drivers license and/or vehicle registration is not readily accessible, do not reach under the seats and do not open the glove box or other compartments and begin searching for your license or registration unless you are asked to do so by the officer. Remain calm and refrain from engaging in sudden or unnecessary movements during the traffic stop.

- Do not talk on a cell phone while interacting with the officer during the stop. The officer has to be able to give you and your passengers detailed instructions so you will understand what is expected of you. If you receive a telephone call during the traffic stop, the officer will tell you whether or not you may answer the telephone call.

- Listen carefully to the officer and follow his or her instructions. Give the officer your full attention. If you do not understand an instruction, calmly inform the officer that you do not understand the instruction and ask him or her to repeat or explain their instruction.

- When the officer completes his or her interaction with you he or she may issue a warning or a traffic ticket which may include a fine. The officer will typically explain whatever action is being taken. If you have questions, respectfully ask the officer to clarify. If you disagree with the officer's decision to issue a traffic ticket, do not prolong the contact by arguing with the officer. If you wish to contest the ticket, you will have the opportunity to explain your point of view of what happened in court. Your acceptance and signature on a traffic ticket is not an admission of guilt.

- Some traffic stops may result in an arrest. Even if you disagree with the officer, do not argue with the officer. You will have your chance to present your case in court. Resisting, delaying or obstructing a law enforcement officer during a traffic stop is a class 2 misdemeanor. N.C.G.S. §14-223.

- If you believe the officer acted inappropriately, document the officer's behavior and report it to the officer's agency in a timely manner. The name of the officer and law enforcement agency will be on the ticket and you may ask the officer to provide this information.

The Law Enforcement Officer

- The officer will initiate a traffic stop by turning on the blue lights and/or siren. The officer is also gathering information from your vehicle's license tag and checking the area for a safe place to conduct the traffic stop.

- The officer will approach your vehicle and will identify himself or herself, his or her agency and the reason for the traffic stop. Many times the officer will ask if you have any reason for committing the traffic violation.

- The officer will ask for your drivers license and the vehicle registration. If the information from your drivers license and the vehicle information does not match, you may be asked a series of questions.

- It is the goal of law enforcement to protect the public and conduct traffic stops in a manner that protects the safety of everyone involved. Your cooperation with law enforcement is the best way to ensure that your safety, and that of others, is not compromised during the stop.

Safe Driving Around Farm Equipment

The agricultural industry is one of the largest employers in North Carolina. Slow-moving agricultural equipment can be found in all parts of the state, including suburban areas. Caution should be taken when sharing the road with farm equipment.

Most of the crashes that involve farm equipment occur on a clear day, during daylight hours, and/or on a dry surface that is paved. Typical crashes with farm equipment include sideswipes and angle crashes.

These types of crashes typically occur while farm equipment is turning left and another vehicle attempts to pass. In some cases, a machinery operator uses a left-hand signal, and drivers may mistake this as a sign for them to pass. When the farm machinery slows to make the turn, the vehicle following attempts to pass and crashes with the equipment.

When sharing the road with farm equipment, you must obey the rules of the road. It is illegal and very dangerous to pass farm equipment in a no passing zone. Farm equipment may be wider than what is visible from behind and may require ample space in both lanes. Furthermore, it may also be difficult to see traffic approaching in the opposite direction.

The key to safety when sharing the road with farm equipment is to be patient. If farm equipment is causing a delay in traffic, the operator should move off the road at the nearest practical location and allow the traffic to pass. This is the only advisable time to pass farm equipment on public roads.

During the harvesting and planting seasons, farmers work longer hours and are often on the road in the early morning and evening hours. Farm equipment is required to have one front white light as well as a rear red light that is visible for up to 500 feet. Two red reflectors that are at least four inches in diameter can replace the rear red light.

Remember, when approaching farm equipment the closure time is much quicker because of the slow speed of the equipment. Always approach farm equipment with care.

Farm equipment is legally entitled to travel on most roads in North Carolina, except interstates.

Funeral Processions

• Every vehicle in a funeral procession must have its headlights on, and the hazard warning signals must also be on, if so equipped.

• The operator of the lead vehicle must comply with all traffic-control signals. But when the lead vehicle has crossed the intersection in accordance with the traffic-control sign or signal, or when directed to do so by a law enforcement officer or funeral director, or when being led by a law enforcement vehicle, all vehicles in the funeral procession may proceed through the intersection without stopping, while using extra care towards other vehicles or pedestrians.

• All vehicles in a funeral procession must be driven on the right side of the road and shall follow the vehicle ahead as closely as reasonable and prudent.

• The driver of a vehicle going in the opposite direction as a funeral procession may yield to the procession. If the driver chooses to yield, the driver must do so by reducing speed, or by stopping completely off the roadway so that drivers of other vehicles proceeding in the opposite direction of the procession can continue to travel without leaving their lane of traffic.

• The driver of a vehicle traveling in the same direction as the funeral procession shall not pass or attempt to pass the funeral procession, except that the operator of such a vehicle may pass a funeral procession when the highway has been marked for two or more lanes of moving traffic in the same direction of the funeral procession.

• The driver of a vehicle shall not knowingly drive between vehicles in a funeral procession. When a funeral procession is proceeding through a red light, the driver of a vehicle that is not in the procession shall not enter the intersection even if facing a green light, unless it can be done safely and without crossing the path of the procession.

Basic Driving Skills and Rules

Driving on Your Side of the Road

The law requires you to drive on the right side of the road. Driving on the left side is legal only in some cases, such as on one-way streets and while passing. When you are moving slower than the posted speed limit on a multi-lane highway, drive in the extreme right lane unless you are passing, turning left or avoiding an obstruction.

Adjusting Your Speed to Driving Conditions

The speed at which you drive determines the distance required to stop your vehicle. Stopping distance also depends on your reaction time. Stopping distances are longer at higher speeds because a vehicle travels farther during the driver's reaction time, and it takes more braking distance to come to a full stop. Even with ideal conditions, if you are traveling 55 miles per hour your vehicle requires approximately 211 feet to stop completely.

Driving at a high speed is dangerous because each additional mile traveled per hour reduces the driver's ability to control the vehicle. Speed also increases the likelihood that a crash will result in serious injury or death. On the other hand, driving below the posted speed limit can also be dangerous. If you must drive slower, you should still observe the posted minimum speed limit. At places where it is unsafe to pass, the slow driver forces other drivers to creep along behind or take unnecessary risks while trying to pass. Very slow driving is especially dangerous just after you have passed the crest of a hill or rounded a curve. Faster-moving vehicles can crash into the slower vehicle before they can slow down. For this reason, watch for slow-moving vehicles such as heavy trucks or farm vehicles. If traffic is collecting behind you, it is wise to pull over to the side of the road, stop and allow the vehicles to pass.

The most important rules about speed are:

> Studies show that the vehicle moving at a speed considerably below the posted limit is much more likely to cause or be involved in a crash than the vehicle moving at a normal speed.

- Never drive faster than the posted speed limit or at a speed that is unreasonable or unwise given the existing conditions.
- Allow a safe distance between you and the vehicle in front of you (the "two-second rule").
- The faster you are moving, the farther ahead you must be able to see to allow enough distance for stopping.

Conditions often change as you drive. You will drive through different areas such as open country, residential communities and school zones. Watch for changing conditions and adjust your speed accordingly.

Unless otherwise posted, the speed limit is 35 mph in cities and towns. Special speed limits may be posted for special areas. To be a safe driver, you must often drive slower than the posted limit, but you should not drive faster.

Maximum Speed Limits

In cities and towns	35
For school buses	45
For school activity buses	55
Outside cities and towns	55
For interstates	70

Rounding a Curve

The best way to handle a curve:

1. Slow down before you enter the curve so that you will not need to brake while you are in the curve;

2. Gradually increase your speed to maintain the traction necessary for good control of the vehicle as you round the curve;

3. If you must brake in the curve, apply the brakes gradually until you are sure it is safe to keep continuous pressure on the brake pedal;

4. Begin to turn the vehicle just prior to the point where the road begins to turn; and

5. Stay on your side of the road and drive as far to the right as you can.

If you encounter a curve while traveling downhill:
1. Consider the pull of gravity;

2. Shift to a lower gear before moving downhill; and

3. Begin to brake earlier and approach the curve more slowly than you would on a level roadway.

Turning

For right turns, stay close to the right edge of the road, so that another vehicle cannot move between your vehicle and the curb. Reduce the vehicle's speed before making the turn and then accelerate slightly.

Motorcycles and bicycles are especially hard to see during a turn. Always give the proper signal and look before turning to make sure that you can turn safely.

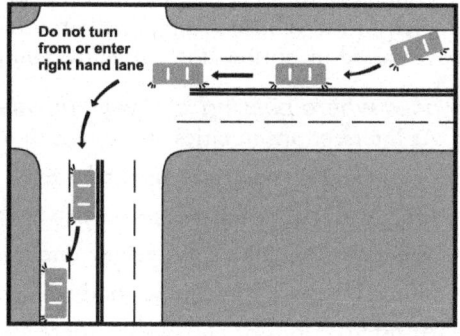

Following

Following too closely is a leading cause of traffic crashes. Maintain plenty of space between your vehicle and the one ahead. If the vehicle ahead stops suddenly, you will need time to react. On the open road, keep enough distance between you and the vehicle ahead so that a passing vehicle can safely move into and occupy the space. Remember to follow the "two-second rule."

The Two-Second Rule

The "two-second rule" says that you should allow two seconds between the time the vehicle ahead of you passes a given point and the time your vehicle reaches the same point.

Changing Lanes

On a highway with multiple lanes of traffic, check the lane you are changing to, as well as the lane beyond, to be certain that another vehicle is not planning to move into the same space.

> **Important rules about changing lanes:**
> - Check the side and rear-view mirrors;
> - Check over your shoulder to be certain the blind spot is clear;
> - Signal your intended movement in advance; and
> - Proceed with changing lanes.

Passing

1. Look ahead and behind to determine when it is safe to pass.
2. If it is safe to pass, signal to alert the drivers ahead and behind you of your intention so they can plan their moves accordingly.
3. Blow the horn to signal the driver ahead.

The horn signal places the driver of the vehicle you are passing under a legal obligation to help you pass. While passing, be sure you have plenty of room and keep a steady speed. You cannot pass safely unless you can see far enough ahead to ensure that you can get back to the original lane of travel before you meet oncoming traffic. The law requires the passing driver to pass at least two feet to the left of the vehicle being passed. You have not passed safely if the vehicle you have passed must slow down to allow you back into your correct lane.

Places where passing is always unsafe and usually illegal:
- At intersections in cities and towns or at railroad crossings;
- At marked intersections in rural areas;
- On any curve or hill where the driver cannot see at least 500 feet ahead;
- Wherever there is a solid yellow line in the driver's lane;
- Wherever there is a double-solid yellow line;
- At intersections or crosswalks where a vehicle has stopped to allow people to cross the street; and
- Wherever the driver cannot see that the road is clear of traffic far enough ahead to pass safely.

Passing on the right

Passing on the right is against the law except in areas where it is specifically permitted. Passing on the right places your vehicle on the blind side of the vehicle you are passing. The vehicle you are passing could unexpectedly make a right turn or pull over to the right side of the road.

Exceptions where passing on the right is allowed:
- On highways having at least two lanes traveling in each direction;
- On one-way streets where all lanes of traffic move in the same direction;
- When passing a vehicle that is in the left-turn lane; and/or
- When driving in a lane set aside for right turns.

On three-lane highways, you must not pass except in the center lane, and then only where the center lane is marked for passing in your direction. *Exception: When the vehicle in the center lane is making a left turn.*

When your vehicle is being passed

When you are being passed, you are required to help the other driver to pass. If the driver of the passing vehicle blows the horn, move to the right edge of the road. Never increase your speed.

If you increase speed and fail to give way to a passing vehicle, you will be charged with a misdemeanor if a crash occurs resulting in bodily injury or property damage.

Backing

Rules to follow when backing your vehicle:

1. Before entering your vehicle, check behind it for small objects or children — once you are in the driver's seat, it is hard to see them;

2. To maintain a full view of what is behind the vehicle, steer with your left hand and look over your right shoulder through the back window — do not depend on mirrors alone or looking through the side window;

3. Back very slowly, not more than 10 mph — your vehicle is harder to control and to stop when it is backing.

Parking

Always park on the right side of the road, except on one-way streets.

Before pulling out from a parallel parking space, check for approaching traffic and give a left-turn signal, unless you are parked on the left side of a one-way street.

If you are driving and notice that a vehicle ahead of you is pulling out from a parallel parking space, slow down and be prepared to stop.

Places where you should not park:
- At an intersection or in front of a driveway;
- Within 25 feet of the curb line of an intersecting street or within 15 feet of the intersecting right of way lines if there is no curb;
- On a crosswalk, sidewalk or bridge;
- Within 15 feet of a fire hydrant or entrance to a fire station;
- On the paved or primary-travel portion of any highway — parking on the shoulder is also against the law unless the parked vehicle can be seen by approaching drivers from both directions for a distance of at least 200 feet;
- On the roadway side of another vehicle (double parking);
- Where there are "no-parking" signs;
- Within one block of a fire or fire truck in city limits or within 400 feet of a fire or fire truck outside the city;
- Anywhere within the right of way of an interstate highway, except in designated parking areas or in cases of emergencies; and
- Parking spaces designated for handicap/disabled use unless your vehicle is displaying a handicap license plate or a disability parking placard. For information about Americans with Disabilities Act, visit *www.ada.gov*.

Special Driving Situations

Interchanges, Intersections, Roads, Streets and Highways

Many intersections may have roads crossing each other at different levels. These are interchanges and the method of turning at these specially designed intersections may vary. As you approach an interchange, slow down and give careful attention to the signs that direct you about how to make the turn. An intersection is any place where two or more roads meet or cross each other. Crashes occur most frequently at intersections, and they are considered the most dangerous places on a street or highway. More than one-third of fatal traffic crashes involving motor vehicles occur at intersections.

On four-lane highways separated by a median of more than 30 feet, each crossing constitutes a separate intersection. The law requires that you slow down when you come to an intersection, even if you have the right of way.

In intersections without traffic signs or signals, the right-of-way rules state:

- The vehicle already in the intersection has the right of way ahead of any vehicle that has not yet entered;

- When two or more vehicles reach an intersection at the same time, the vehicle to the right has the right of way;

- A vehicle with the right-of-way may move straight ahead or, if legal and after signaling, turn right or left; and

- Even with the right-of-way, be careful to avoid hitting other vehicles and pedestrians.

> ## TIP
> ### Single-Point Interchange
> A single-point interchange compresses two intersections into a single intersection over or under a free-flowing road. Through traffic and traffic turning left onto or off the interchange, is controlled by a single set of traffic signals. The traffic signals are located at the center or top of the interchange and allow vehicles to clear the intersection more quickly. These interchanges help move large volumes of traffic through limited amounts of space safely and efficiently.

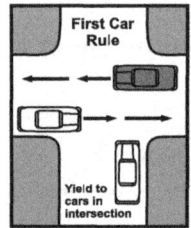
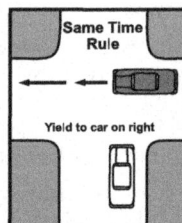
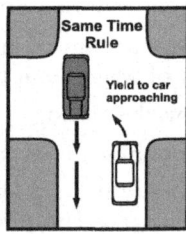

When two facing vehicles approach an intersection at the same time, the right-of-way rules are not much help. Both drivers can move straight ahead or turn right. If one driver is going straight while the other wants to turn left, the driver who wants to turn must wait. The driver who wants to turn left must give the proper signal and wait until the turn can be made safely. Therefore, in this case, the driver who is traveling straight ahead has the right of way. Never change lanes while you are moving straight ahead through an intersection.

Right-of-Way at Intersections

When you approach an intersection with a stop sign, you must come to a complete stop and yield to the traffic on the through-street. Do not move ahead or turn until you can proceed safely.

Drive with caution at intersections with traffic signals and wait until the signal permits you to turn or to move straight ahead.

When exiting a private driveway, stop and yield to all other vehicles and pedestrians. At unmarked intersections where it is hard to see in all directions, stop and then move forward slowly and cautiously.

Railroad Crossing Safety

§ 20-142.1. Obedience to railroad signal.

(a) Whenever any person driving a vehicle approaches a railroad grade crossing under any of the circumstances stated in this section, the driver of the vehicle shall stop within 50 feet, but not less than 15 feet from the nearest rail of the railroad and shall not proceed until he can do so safely. These requirements apply when:

(1) A clearly visible electrical or mechanical signal device gives warning of the immediate approach of a railroad train;

(2) A crossing gate is lowered or when a human flagman gives or continues to give a signal of the approach or passage of a railroad train;

(3) A railroad train approaching within approximately 1500 feet of the highway crossing emits a signal audible from that distance, and the railroad train is an immediate hazard because of its speed or nearness to the crossing; or

(4) An approaching railroad train is plainly visible and is in hazardous proximity to the crossing.

(b) No person shall drive any vehicle through, around, or under any crossing gate or barrier at a railroad crossing while the gate or barrier is closed or is being opened or closed, nor shall any pedestrian pass through, around, over, or under any crossing gate or barrier at a railroad crossing while the gate or barrier is closed or is being opened or closed.

(c) When stopping as required at a railroad crossing, the driver shall keep as far to the right of the highway as possible and shall not form two lanes of traffic unless the roadway is marked for four or more lanes of traffic.

(d) Any person who violates any provisions of this section shall be guilty of an infraction and punished in accordance with G.S. 20-176. Violation of this section shall not constitute negligence per se.

> ## TIP
> ### *Traffic Circles and Roundabouts*
>
> A traffic circle or roundabout is a specially designed intersection. All vehicles in a traffic circle travel to the right around the circle in a counterclockwise direction until you come to the road or street where you want to turn. You leave the traffic circle by making a right turn. If there is more than one lane in the circle, be sure you are in the outside lane before you come to the place where you intend to exit the circle. Look and signal before you turn or change lanes. Never make a right turn from an inside lane. *An entire traffic circle is an intersection. Vehicles already in the circle have the right of way.*

> **There are over 5000 miles of railroad tracks and 6800 railroad crossings in N.C.**
> **A train that is traveling at 55 mph takes more than a mile to come to a stop**

(e) An employer who knowingly allows, requires, permits, or otherwise authorizes a driver of a commercial motor vehicle to violate this section shall be guilty of an infraction. Such employer will also be subject to a civil penalty under G.S. 20-37.21. (1991, c. 368, s. 1; 2005-349, s. 12.)

A yellow and black "RR" sign indicates that you are approaching a railroad crossing. As you approach the tracks, look both ways and listen because you may have to stop. Trains can approach a crossing at any time from any direction. The train always has the right of way. If there is a stop sign, you must come to a full stop before safely crossing.

> Trains have the right-of-way over all highway traffic including police, fire and ambulance emergency vehicles.

A railroad crossing sign indicates you are approaching a railroad crossing and you must:

• Approach with caution

• Prepare to stop and be alert for a train

• Proceed with caution after a train has passed

• Never stop on train tracks for any reason

The X-shaped railroad grade crossing sign, known as a Crossbuck Sign is mounted at the railroad crossing. A smaller sign below the crossbuck indicates if there is more than one track.

Many crossings have flashing red lights or flashing red lights with gates. If the warning signal activates, you must stop before the gates lower across your side of the road. **It is unlawful and extremely dangerous to move through a railroad crossing when the gates are lowered. You will not be able to cross the tracks before the train arrives and the train cannot turn and will not be able to stop.**

> **As you approach a railroad crossing, you must:**
> • Slow your speed;
> • Look both ways;
> • Listen for the train;
> • Keep alert; and
> • Watch for the railroad crossing signal.

Remember these railroad crossing rules:

• Railroads are private property and it is illegal and dangerous to drive on or cross the tracks except at designated railroad crossings;

• Vehicles must always yield to a train even when the crossing only has a crossbuck and no lights or gates;

• When flashing red lights are used with crossbuck signs at the railroad crossing, you must stop, just as you would stop for any flashing red traffic signal;

• If you are waiting for a train to pass, be patient;

- Do not proceed to move immediately after the train has passed — there may be another train moving in the opposite direction from or following the first train;

- Always wait until the red lights have stopped flashing before moving ahead;

- Be prepared to stop for vehicles that must stop at crossings, such as school buses, motor vehicles carrying passengers, for-hire vehicles or vehicles transporting explosives or hazardous materials (these vehicles are marked with placards). If you happen to be crossing the tracks and the warning lights begin flashing or gates start to come down, do not stop, do not backup, KEEP MOVING. The warning signals will allow enough time for you to finish driving through the crossing before the train arrives. If the gate on the far side of the tracks comes down before you get across, DO NOT PANIC. RAILROAD CROSSING GATES CANNOT TRAP YOU OR YOUR VEHICLE drive through the gate. It is flexible and will not block you in. If you stop and try to back up, your vehicle may stall;

- Crossing gates will not trap you, but stopping traffic might. Be sure the traffic ahead of you will not stop and block you in on the tracks;

Railroad related emergencies: What you need to know.

REPORT EMERGENCY
OR PROBLEM
1–800–XXX–XXXX
X-ING 999 999 Z

Railroad Emergency Notification System sign, also known as the Blue Sign.

Knowing how to use the Blue Sign to directly contact the railroad company is the quickest method to stop a train in the event of a railroad related emergency.

An example (above) of the railroad Emergency Notification Sign (Blue Sign) and its location is depicted in the red circle on the illustration below.

- All highway-railroad crossings in North Carolina are required to have an Emergency Notification System (ENS) sign posted in each traffic direction. The ENS sign, known as the "Blue sign," contains the railroad crossing identification number, name of the railroad company and an emergency telephone number to report emergencies, hazardous conditions or issues with railroad crossing lights or gates directly to the railroad company. Familiarize yourself with the "Blue Sign "locations at railroad crossings during your travels.

- Each railroad company has its own emergency telephone number and each railroad crossing has a unique USDOT crossing identification number.

- If your vehicle stalls on or near the tracks GET OUT IMMEDIATELY. A train, which may weigh several thousand tons traveling at 55 mph may take more than a mile to stop. By the time the engineer on the train sees you, it is too late to stop the train.

- Move away from your vehicle and the tracks. Walk quickly along the roadway to a safe location away from the railroad tracks.

- When you are safely away from the tracks, locate the Blue Sign located at or near the railroad crossing and report the emergency.

> When a train hits a 4,000-lb. car, it is like your car running over a soda can. No vehicle is worth a life.

With rail traffic increasing throughout North Carolina, it is more important than ever to practice safety at railroad crossings. Trains cannot stop quickly, but your vehicle can.

Bicycle Lanes

When a bicycle lane or bike path travels on or adjacent to the roadway, please pay special attention to bicyclists as you approach and move through an intersection. Because bicyclists ride to the right of motor vehicle traffic, the potential exists for a crash between the bicyclist who is moving straight ahead through the intersection and the motorist who is turning right.

City Driving

Driving in cities and towns can pose problems for some drivers. Traffic is often heavy in urban areas. Watch for approaching traffic at side streets. When driving in heavy traffic, be alert for drivers who make quick stops. To avoid a rear-end crash by another vehicle, check your rear-view mirror often and stay aware of dangerous situations that might exist behind you. If you intend to make a turn and find that you are not in the proper lane, continue to the next intersection and turn there.

Other rules to follow when driving in cities:
- Give yourself plenty of space to make decisions — leave a "margin of safety" around your vehicle;
- Communicate your intended movements to other drivers;
- Watch the road far enough ahead of you to detect possibly dangerous situations earlier and to take proper defensive actions;
- Avoid driving side-by-side, especially in another driver's blind spot — if you cannot see the inside rear-view mirror of the car ahead, you are probably in the driver's blind spot;
- Never "weave" in and out of traffic — stay in one lane if you can and plan lane changes ahead of time;
- Give proper signal in advance before changing lanes;
- Be prepared to apply the brakes;
- Watch for parked vehicles that might be pulling out and pedestrians who might dart onto the street from between parked vehicles. Parked vehicles can also block your view of intersecting traffic, driveways and alleys; and
- On a one-way street, use the center lane(s) for through-travel and the outside lanes for turning.

Open Roads

Rural highways can be narrow two-lane roads or multi-lane highways.

Driving on rural roads is often more dangerous than driving in heavy city traffic because:
- The road may not be as wide;
- The lighting is often not as good; and/or
- The travel speeds may be higher.
- Stay alert for drivers who might be driving slower than the posted speed limit.

Secondary Roads

A paved secondary road is not always designed for heavy traffic or regular highway speed. Most secondary roads are built for local transportation, and not as main highways. On these roads, hills are likely to be steeper and curves are likely to be sharper than on primary roads. Sight distances are often very short. Secondary roads cannot be traveled safely at speeds that would be proper for primary highways.

Interstate Highways

Interstate highways are safer roads because they have separate traffic lanes for vehicles moving in opposite directions and fewer places where traffic can enter and exit. Also, interstates do not have railroad crossings, sharp curves, stop signs or traffic signals.

For information about North Carolina's new toll roads, call the N.C. Quick Pass office at 1-877-769-7277 or visit ***www.myncquickpass.com***.

When driving on an interstate, follow these rules:
- Plan your trip in advance;
- Be sure to check the vehicle's water, oil, tires and gas before leaving on your trip;
- Decide in advance where you must enter and exit the highway;
- When entering the interstate, use the acceleration lane until your vehicle's speed matches that of the other traffic and then merge safely;
- Keep to the right, use the left lane(s) for passing;
- Do not tailgate. Keep a safe following distance for the speed you are traveling — one of the most frequent types of crashes on an interstate highway is the rear–end crash — use the "two-second rule";
- Remember that faster speeds require greater stopping distances and times;
- Stop at indicated rest areas frequently, preferably at least once every 100 miles;
- Never stop in the travel lane;
- If a vehicle breakdown forces you to stop, move far off the road. Tie a white cloth on the radio aerial or left-door handle and raise the hood. If the breakdown occurs at night, engage the vehicle's emergency flashers or parking lights. If you are a driver who spots a vehicle breakdown, immediately contact the N.C. State Highway Patrol or local law enforcement; and
- When leaving the highway, signal your turn well in advance, and without

slowing down, enter the deceleration lane. Proceed at the posted exit speed limit.

Remember these tips when you drive:
- As your speed increases, look farther ahead.
- Give particular attention to hidden intersections and driveways.
- Watch for warning signs that signal changes in the road.
- Watch for other vehicles, especially oversized and slow-moving ones.
- Maintain a safe following distance.
- Use the vehicle's headlights when visibility becomes poor.
- Be especially alert to oncoming vehicles because they are only a few feet away on some two-lane, undivided highways.
- If you see a line of vehicles approaching, watch for drivers who might be trying to pass.
- Always have a possible "escape route" to avoid colliding with an oncoming vehicle.
- Keep aware of vehicles in the lanes next to you.

Traffic moves much faster on the interstate than on an ordinary highway. It is dangerous to drive very far below the posted speed limit. Follow the flow of traffic if you can do so without speeding. Crashes are more likely to occur when a vehicle moves significantly slower than the flow of the traffic.

> If you enter an interstate headed in the wrong direction, pull over to the right shoulder of the road and stop. When the way is clear, turn around and head in the proper direction.
> (Avoid this error by watching for DO NOT ENTER signs.)

Entering and Exiting the Interstate

A dangerous error made by drivers on an interstate is to attempt to leave the highway after missing an exit. If you miss an exit, do not slow down, back up or try to turn around. Proceed to the next exit and leave the highway there instead. You can always find a service or side street to return to your intended exit.

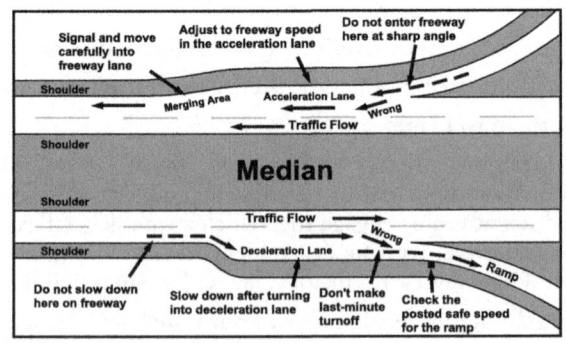

Vehicle Equipment

> To drive safely, all vehicle equipment should be in good working order.

Lights

Make sure all the lights on your vehicle work.

- When you engage the high-beam headlights at night, you should be able to see a person who is 200 feet away. When using the low-beam headlights, you should be able to see someone who is 75 feet away.
- When headlights are improperly adjusted, they can shine in the eyes of approaching drivers, bicyclists and pedestrians. Vehicle vibration can cause the headlights to become out of adjustment.
- It is a good practice to routinely check and adjust the headlights.
- Overloading the rear of your vehicle may cause the front of your vehicle to tilt and produce an uncomfortable and sometimes hazardous headlight glare for oncoming drivers, bicyclists and pedestrians.
- Taillights must be red in color and visible for at least 500 feet.
- The law requires a white light shining on the license plate to make the numbers visible for at least 50 feet.
- All motor vehicles produced since 1955 must have red or amber lights that engage when the brakes or turn signals are used — these lights may be combined with the taillights or may be separated, and they must be visible for at least 100 feet in normal daylight.
- Because hand signals are difficult to see at night, it is important that a vehicle's lights have clean lenses and stay in proper working order.

Mirrors

Check and adjust the mirrors before you begin to drive. The rear-view mirror should show what is directly behind you. Adjust the side mirrors to show the scene to the left and right rear of the vehicle. The mirrors should barely reflect the side of the vehicle.

Brakes

- Every motor vehicle that operates on a public roadway must be equipped with brakes to adequately control the movement of, stop and hold the vehicle.
- All vehicles should have originally equipped brakes in good working condition — having two separate means of applying the brakes.
- The brake pedal should be at least one-third of its original distance from the floor when fully depressed. If it is not, the brakes must be checked and, if necessary, repaired.
- If the pedal gradually lowers under the pressure of your foot, the hydraulic system must be checked.
- Brakes that squeak when you depress the brake pedal can indicate a problem, have them checked. Do not risk a possible loss of the brakes.

Anti-lock Braking System

Anti-lock brakes, or ABS, can help improve vehicle stability (avoiding spin-outs), steerability (directing the vehicle where the driver wants it to go) and stopping capability (distance needed to stop the vehicle).

With ABS, it is important to brake hard and keep firm and steady pressure on the brake pedal while stopping. Pumping the brake pedal or releasing the steady pressure on the brake pedal will reduce the effectiveness of the ABS.

Auto Theft Prevention

To help prevent auto theft, never leave the key in the ignition switch of an unattended vehicle.

Tires

Every vehicle operated on the streets and highways of North Carolina must be equipped with tires that are safe for the operation of the vehicle and do not expose the public to needless hazards. Tires are considered unsafe if they are cut, cracked or worn so as to expose the tire cord, or when they have visible tread separation, chunking or less than 1/16-inch-tread depth.

Tires are important for stopping your vehicle. Never drive on smooth tires or tires that have fabric showing. Tires without enough air wear out more quickly. Also, tires without enough air increase the likelihood of a blowout. Over-inflated tires reduce traction and wear heavily on the middle of the tread.

The air pressure of tires must be checked at least once each month. For safe driving and fuel economy, tires should have the right amount of air. Follow the manufacturer's recommendation. The best time to check air pressure is when the tires are cool. If you do not have an air pressure gauge, you can take your vehicle to a nearby service station or auto center to have it checked.

Horns and Sirens

Only law enforcement and emergency vehicles may have emergency lights or sirens.

- Every licensed motor vehicle must be equipped with a horn in good working order.
- The horn must be loud enough to be heard for at least 200 feet, and it must not make any unreasonably loud or harsh sound.
- If the horn fails, have it repaired immediately.
- The horn must be used as a reasonable warning device. You should not use the horn unnecessarily or unreasonably.

Muffler and Exhaust System

Every motor vehicle must have a muffler that is in good working order. The muffler filters smoke and excessive noise. One function of the exhaust system is to take harmful fumes from the engine to the rear of the vehicle to be released. Check your exhaust system often to be sure it is not leaking. A leak in the exhaust system can allow poisonous carbon monoxide gas to enter the passenger compartment of the vehicle. Carbon monoxide poisoning often can be fatal, and even small amounts can cause you to become sleepy or unconscious and lose control of the vehicle. For this reason, it is suggested that you keep a window open about one inch while traveling.

Suspension System

If a vehicle sways freely, leans heavily to one side during a turn or seems to bounce continuously, there may be a problem with the suspension system. Have a mechanic inspect the suspension system, including shock absorbers, and immediately correct any defects. A faulty suspension system can cause you to lose control of the vehicle.

Emergency Warning Flashers

Vehicles are equipped with an emergency warning device that flashes all four turn signal lights. These flashers can be used as a warning by any vehicle to signal other drivers of a possible danger or that a vehicle is stopped or disabled.

Drive Green

Driving green means adopting a few simple, inexpensive driving habits to decrease the amount of fuel you use and put more money in your pocket.

- When you carry extra weight, your vehicle must work harder.
- Check tire pressure once a month and keep tires properly inflated.
- Every five miles over 60 mph can cost you up to an additional 30 cents a gallon.
- Abrupt starts and hard stops can increase fuel consumption by 40%.
- Turn off the engine if you're waiting for more than a couple of minutes.
- At speeds less than 40 mph, roll down windows; more than 40 mph, use AC.
- Use the cruise control for more than 10,000 miles a year and save yourself 60 gallons of fuel.
- Clogged air filters can cut mileage by 10%.
- Tightening your fuel cap can prevent leakage of up to 30 gallons of gas a year.

Defensive Driving

Driving involves two important types of skills:
- Skills that enable the driver to drive defensively and to avoid a crash in spite of driving errors by others; and
- Skills for the basic rules about turning, passing, backing and parking the vehicle.

Scanning

What you see is important for defensive driving.

- Good drivers try to see 10 to 15 seconds ahead on the roadway (about one city block). By looking ahead, you might avoid last minute moves such as sudden stops or quick lane changes.
- About every 10 seconds check the mirrors to see if any vehicle is following too closely.

- When changing lanes, backing, slowing down or driving down a long hill, it is important to check for traffic from behind the car and in your blind spots.
- While checking the mirrors, do not take your eyes off the road for more than an instant. The vehicle in front of you could stop suddenly.
- Always leave yourself an "out."

Although mirrors are useful, you should remember they do not show the full picture. Mirrors leave "blind" spots in your field of vision. "Blind" spots are the areas near the left and right rear corners of the vehicle that you cannot see using the mirrors from the driver's perspective. Therefore, before you make any lane changes or turns, quickly turn your head and look over your shoulder to see what is in the blind spot. Additional blind spots can be created by glaring lights, dirty windshields, vehicles parked too closely to an intersection, bushes and/or buildings. In these cases, ease your vehicle forward until you can see clearly. Avoid driving in other drivers' blind spots where it is more difficult for them to see you.

Communicating

Communicating means letting others know what you plan to do early enough to avoid a crash. Anytime you plan to slow down, stop, turn, change lanes or pull away from the curb, you should signal your intention. Be in the habit of signalling your movements even when you do not see others on the road. Before you signal, you must first see that your movement can be made safely.

Hand Signals

> **Hand signals are given from the driver's window, using the left arm and hand:**
> - To signal a left turn, hold the arm and hand straight out and point the first finger.
> - To signal a right turn, hold the arm straight out and the forearm and hand straight up, palm facing forward.
> - To signal stopping and slowing down, point the arm and hand down, palm facing back.

Flashing Turn Signals

Flashing light signals for turns are legal substitutes for hand signals, but there are times when they are hard to see. In late afternoon and early morning, the lenses may reflect sunlight, making it difficult to tell whether the signals are flashing. At night a flashing light signal is much easier to see than a hand signal. Use the type of signal you believe will communicate best. The flashing light signal is sufficient at night. Signal at least the last 100 feet before turning or stopping. If the speed limit is 45 mph or more, signal at least the last 200 feet before turning. The faster you are driving, the farther ahead you should signal.

Keeping a Margin of Safety

Allow a margin of safety around you by staying clear of other vehicles. Make sure there is enough room ahead and behind to pass or stop safely.

Drive at a steady speed, and signal well in advance whenever you are slowing down or stopping to warn other drivers from following too closely. If another vehicle follows you too closely, move to another lane and signal for the driver to pass you. Stay in the middle of the lane and leave space on both sides of your vehicle. Allow ample room between your vehicle, parked vehicles and oncoming traffic.

Adjusting

Adjusting to road conditions is the key to successful driving.

• You should be able to judge dangerous conditions and adjust your driving accordingly.

• Most importantly, you should know when conditions are too dangerous to risk driving at all.

In situations when you have to deal with two or more unavoidable dangers at the same time, adjust by giving the most room to the greatest or most likely danger. Suppose there are approaching vehicles to your left and a child on a bicycle to your right. The child is most likely to make a sudden move, so give the child more room. This may mean moving closer to the oncoming vehicles. If the dangers are equally hazardous, such as oncoming vehicles and parked vehicles, you should stop and allow the oncoming vehicles to pass safely before proceeding.

Hazardous Driving

Work Zones

A street or highway work zone warns of construction or maintenance activities

that are on or adjacent to the road used by vehicles. The work zone may or may not actually interfere with the normal traffic flow, but it will usually contain activities that may tend to draw the driver's attention or otherwise distract a driver from traffic. It is very important to STAY ALERT in work zones and to be prepared at all times to react safely to unexpected conditions.

It is unlawful to drive a motor vehicle greater than the speed limit that is set and posted while driving in a work zone. A highway work zone is the area between the first sign that indicates the beginning of a work zone and the last sign that indicates the end of a work zone. There is a penalty for speeding in a work zone if a sign is posted at the beginning of the work zone listing the penalty. This penalty is in addition to any other penalties for the speeding conviction. A highway work zone can be easily identified by unique orange warning signs immediately preceding the work zone. The orange signs with messages in black letters are reserved strictly to identify work zones. In addition to alerting drivers as they approach and enter work zones, black-on-orange signs are used within the work zone to convey specific information and directions to drivers as they travel through the work zone.

Warning signs alert drivers of unusual features or conditions that they are about to encounter.

Examples of typical work zone signs:

The "Flagger" sign warns drivers of construction or maintenance on the road ahead where a flagger wearing an orange vest is stationed at the site to control traffic. The flagger uses a "STOP/SLOW" paddle to either stop traffic or allow traffic to proceed. When you see the "Flagger" sign, STAY ALERT and be prepared to stop.

When driving in a work zone:
- Recognize that when you see black-on-orange signs, you are about to enter a work zone and should STAY ALERT.
- Advance work zone signs may require you to take some action like shifting your vehicle to another lane.
- When you are required to take action, black-on-orange signs will convey the message far in advance, so you will have enough time to take the action.
- Do not wait until the last minute to take action — the signs provide sufficient time for the driver to react without impeding traffic.

Driving slower than the surrounding traffic is a major cause of rear-end crashes in work zones. In the work zone, driving areas may be confined, and there may be no maneuvering space or escape route for vehicles that unexpectedly approach a slow-moving vehicle ahead. Traffic control devices such as barricades, cones, drums, flaggers, etc. are used in work zones to guide and direct drivers safely through the area.

Night Driving
The law requires use of headlights from sunset to sunrise and when visibility is 400 feet or less. When you drive at night in a city, use low-beam headlights. On the open road, use high-beam headlights unless you are approaching or following another vehicle.

Night driving is more dangerous than daytime driving because:
- You cannot see as well;

- There are more impaired drivers on the road;

- Drivers tend to be tired and less alert;

- A driver can be blinded by the headlights of oncoming vehicles; and

- Dirty windshields and poor lights can cause problems for some drivers.

Tips for nighttime driving:
- When an approaching vehicle does not dim its headlights, you can remind the driver by blinking your high beams once;

- If the driver still does not dim the lights, keep your lights on low beam;

- Stay on the right side of the road and use the edge of the road as a guide;

- Reduce speed and watch the road as far ahead as possible, looking slightly to the right so you will not be looking directly into the headlights of oncoming traffic;

- Never drive at a speed at which you cannot stop within the distance you can see on the road ahead; and

- Keep a lookout at all times — bright headlights from another vehicle make it difficult to see beyond their source.

- When parking on or along a highway, turn on your emergency flashers;

- Never leave your headlights on when you park at night — they can blind the drivers of oncoming vehicles.

Sun Glare

Sunlight, either direct or reflected, poses a dangerous driving situation for drivers. To reduce this problem, adjust your sun visor and wear sunglasses. If these do not help, stop on the roadside until you can drive safely.

Rain

Rain reduces visibility and makes pavement dangerous. You may be able to see only a few feet ahead; therefore, you should drive more slowly than usual, **and you must use your headlights and windshield wipers.** Stopping distances on slippery pavement increases from two to 10 times farther than on dry pavement; therefore, slow down and allow yourself at least twice the normal following distance.

Roads are more dangerous just after rain has begun to fall, especially if it has not rained for a while. For the first 10 to 15 minutes, rain combines with oil from asphalt and vehicles, and with dirt, dust and rubber to create a slick surface. You should drive with extreme caution. Drive at least five to 10 miles per hour slower on wet pavement than you would on dry pavement. You must also be prepared if your vehicle hydroplanes.

Hydroplaning

Hydroplaning occurs when a thin sheet of water gets between the road surface and a vehicle's tires, causing them to lose contact with the road. The vehicle then begins a skidding movement across the road. Hydroplaning can start at speeds as low as 30 miles per hour and in water little more than 1/8 inch deep. When your speed increases, so do the chances of hydroplaning. Your ability to stop, or even slow your vehicle, is greatly reduced. Once you begin to hydroplane, any sudden jerking of the steering wheel or even a strong gust of wind can send you into an uncontrollable skid that can result in a crash. If you do begin to hydroplane, take your foot off the gas pedal. *Resist your instinct to use the brakes.* Keep your steering wheel straight and let the car's momentum decrease until the tires grip the road again and you regain control.

Before going out in rainy weather, check your tires. Tires with deep, open treads allow water to escape and help prevent hydroplaning at moderate speeds. Tires with worn tread and those that are under inflated have less grip on the road surface, increasing your chance of hydroplaning. To properly handle skids, it is better to have tire pressure on the high side, rather than the low side, of the manufacturer's specifications.

Be alert to warning signs of standing water on the roadway, which can lead to hydroplaning. These include visible reflections on the surface of the water; "dimples" created by rain drops as they hit the water; a "slushing" sound made by your tires; and a "loose" feeling in your steering wheel. If driving after a rainstorm has just ended, continue to be cautious. Rain leaves puddles in the road for several hours, even days after the showers stop, that can cause a car to hydroplane.

Never use cruise control when it is raining or after it has been raining. If your vehicle starts to hydroplane, the time that it takes to turn off the cruise control or tap the brake pedal to release it, could mean the difference in maintaining or losing control of your vehicle.

Driving in Flood Conditions

Since 1970, inland flooding has been responsible for 85 percent of deaths associated with tropical weather in North Carolina. Half of these deaths were caused by people driving into known flooded roads.

Never drive through standing water on a roadway. The water level may be much higher than it appears and it is possible that part of the roadway may be washed away. Take precautions whenever you see water moving across a roadway during or after heavy rains or during flooding conditions. Your vehicle may stall and be swept off the roadway into deeper waters. There have been reports that six inches of fast moving water can sweep a car off the highway and 12 inches of fast moving water can float a car or cause it to turn over.

Windshield Wipers/Headlights

All North Carolina motorists are required to use headlights whenever they are using windshield wipers due to inclement weather.

Fog

If you must drive during fog:
- Turn on the low beam headlights;
- Reduce your driving speed and be alert for tail lights of the vehicle in front of you; and
- Watch for the vehicles behind you.

If you have extreme trouble seeing, you need to:
- Pull far off the roadway;
- Stop, secure the vehicle and turn on its emergency flashers; and
- Leave the vehicle from the passenger side and stay away from the road.

Snow and Ice

Snow and ice make roads very slippery. Hard-packed snow increases the danger of skidding. As you drive, watch for shady spots, bridges and overpasses since these places are often the first to freeze as the temperature drops. If you must drive during a snowstorm, reduce speed, use windshield wipers and turn on the low-beam headlights. It is recommended that you reduce speed by more than half for packed snow and slow to a crawl on ice. Use chains if necessary for better traction, but do not forget that even chains and snow tires can slide on ice and packed snow. You cannot start, stop or maneuver quickly in these conditions. Watch for other drivers, especially those who do not have their vehicles under control.

When you are starting or stopping on snowy or icy roads:
- Increase your speed slowly;
- Get the "feel of the road" by testing your steering control and the braking friction;
- Start to move in second gear or higher and release the clutch slowly (for manual shifts);
- Allow at least three times the normal stopping distance to slow down;
- (When you stop) keep your foot off the brake and let the engine slow the vehicle; and
- Maintain extra distance between yourself and the vehicle in front of you.

Emergencies

It is important to know what to do if you have a mechanical problem or if an unusual situation occurs. Most importantly, do not panic, but react promptly and appropriately to the emergency. Below are some tips and suggestions for dealing with emergency situations.

Brake Failure
- Shift into a lower gear, release the clutch pedal (for manual transmissions) and apply the emergency brake.

- If the vehicle is equipped with automatic transmission, apply the emergency brake and move the gear control lever into the low-range position.

Using the emergency brake in this manner could cause damage to it and the transmission, but under the circumstances of brake failure there is no better choice.

Wet Brakes
You can help to dry the brakes by:
- Driving a short distance; and
- Applying light pressure to the brake pedal.

The heat generated by the friction of the brakes will evaporate the water from the brake linings.

To prevent excessive wear on brakes when moving down a long hill or steep grade, use a lower gear instead of the brake pedal to control speed. It is best to shift to the lower gear at the top of the hill before you descend.

Gas Pedal Sticks
If your gas pedal sticks:
- Tap the gas pedal to try to unstick the throttle linkage or lift the pedal with your foot;
- Shift to neutral and apply firm pressure to the brakes without locking the wheels; and/or
- Find a safe place to move the vehicle completely off the road.

Blowouts
If you begin to feel a bumpy ride when there is no obvious reason, stop and check your tires. You can tell a blowout by a loud noise and by the way the vehicle begins to swerve.

> **If a blowout occurs:**
> - Hold the steering wheel tightly and try to keep the vehicle straight on your side of the road;
> - Reduce speed by lifting your foot from the accelerator;
> - Do not apply the brakes until the engine has slowed the vehicle enough to allow you to maintain control of the vehicle; and
> - Find a safe place to move the vehicle completely off the road.

Use caution before changing a flat tire.
- Move the vehicle completely off the road.
- Set the parking brake and use emergency flares (if you have them) to warn other drivers.
- Direct all passengers to leave the vehicle by the passenger side. Never allow passengers to remain in the vehicle during a tire change. Move passengers off the road or shoulder — do not allow them to stand in front or to the rear of the vehicle.

- Turn on the emergency flashers and parking lights.
- Block the wheels to prevent the vehicle from rolling.

Breakdowns

Do not attempt to make repairs on a vehicle while it is in an area exposed to other traffic. Call a tow truck or mechanic for assistance.

What you should do if your vehicle breaks down:

- Exit the main part of the road — move the vehicle completely onto the shoulder of the road;

- Make sure you leave the vehicle by the passenger side, and do not allow passengers to remain in the vehicle;

- Stand off the road and away from the vehicle — do not stand in front or to the rear of the vehicle;

- If you need help, tie a white cloth to the left door handle or the radio aerial and raise the hood of the vehicle; and

- If it's dark, turn on the parking lights or emergency flashers. Always have flashlights or flares in your vehicle for emergencies.

Unusual Emergencies

An approaching vehicle that crosses the center line into the path of your vehicle is a danger. You should:

- Reduce speed immediately;
- Sound your horn; and
- Keep to the right even if this means running off the road.

Tips to follow if your vehicle runs off the pavement and onto the shoulder:
- Do not immediately apply the brakes or try to turn back; you could skid, lose control or overturn;
- Slowly remove your foot from the accelerator and steer straight ahead;
- Allow the engine to slow the vehicle; and
- When the vehicle is stopped or nearly stopped, check for approaching traffic and if it's safe, gradually drive back onto the road.

Skids

Certain roadway conditions such as wet roads, ice and packed snow are more likely to cause skids.

To avoid skidding when driving with these roadway conditions:
- Reduce speed gradually;
- Engage your anti-lock braking system using firm, steady pressure on the brake pedal. Do not PUMP anti-lock brakes. If you do not have anti-lock brakes, you should pump the brakes gently to slow the vehicle.

If you find yourself in a skid:
- Ease your foot off the accelerator;
- Turn the steering wheel in the direction the rear of the vehicle is skidding; and
- As soon as the vehicle's path begins to straighten, turn the steering wheel back the other way so you will not over-steer.

Crashes

If a crash seems likely:
- Sound the horn;
- Keep to the right;
- Turn away from oncoming traffic, even if you must leave the road; and/or
- Drive off the road, into an open field if possible.

If you are about to be hit from the rear, and there are no vehicles in front of you:
- Press the accelerator and move away as quickly as possible;
- Be ready to apply your brakes if there is no room to move;
- Brace yourself between the steering wheel and the seat; and
- Press the back of your head firmly against the head rest.

If you are about to be hit:
- Keep a tight grip on the steering wheel; and
- Prepare to turn fast so that you can try to control the vehicle.
- If all else fails, use your arms and hands to protect your face from breaking glass.

In the event you are involved in a crash:
- You must stop the vehicle immediately. If you do not stop, you have violated the law;
- Take precautions to prevent further crashes at the scene;
- Do whatever you can to help those who have been injured;
- Try to ensure that someone informs a law enforcement officer immediately; and
- If the crash occurred on a main lane, ramp, shoulder, median or adjacent area of the highway and there are no injuries or fatalities, each vehicle should be moved out of the travel lane onto the shoulder of the road provided it can be driven safely under its own power and without causing further damage to the vehicle, other traffic or the roadway.

The law protects persons who stop and render aid at the scene of an accident from civil liability except for intentional wrongdoing or unruly conduct.

You are required by law to make an immediate report to the nearest law enforcement officer or agency of any crash when any person is killed or injured or the total damage to vehicles and other property appears to amount to $1,000 or more. Failure to make the report may result in prosecution, and your driver license could be suspended. You should also report any crash to your insurance company. In certain cases, North Carolina law also requires the driver of a vehicle involved in a reportable crash to provide proof of financial responsibility (liability insurance) on forms provided by the Division of Motor Vehicles. These forms must be completed and filed with DMV.

Three things you must do if involved in a crash:

- Provide your name, address, driver license number, vehicle registration number and the name of your vehicle insurance company;

- Be sure to obtain the same information from others who were involved in the crash; and

- If you do not know the occupants of the other vehicle or the owner of damaged property, write down all the information you can gather and give it to the nearest law enforcement officer.

Chapter 5

Signals, Signs and Pavement Markings

Traffic signals, signs and pavement markings are used for traffic control to provide a smooth, orderly flow of traffic. It is important to understand their meanings.

Traffic Signals

The traffic signal is used to control traffic and pedestrians at some intersections and mid-block crosswalks.

- A circular green signal means "go," but left turning traffic is "unprotected" and must yield the right of way to oncoming traffic.

- A circular yellow signal means "caution" and indicates that the signal is about to turn red. Stop for a yellow signal unless you are too close to the intersection to stop safely — in that case, drive cautiously through the intersection. Never speed up for a yellow signal to "beat" the red signal.

- A steady red circular signal means "STOP." Unless there is a sign indicating "NO TURN ON RED," a right turn can be made after coming to a complete stop. All vehicles turning right shall yield the right of way to other traffic and pedestrians using the intersection and to pedestrians in reasonably close proximity to the intersection and who are starting to cross in front of the traffic that is required to stop at the red light. Failure to yield to a pedestrian under these circumstances will result in a penalty of not more than $500 and not less than $100.

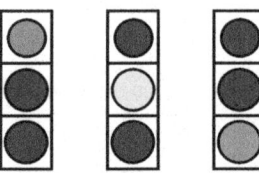

Arrow signals are also important traffic signals.

- A green arrow means that you have a "protected" turning movement with no other conflicting traffic in the intersection except U-turn traffic that should yield to all other traffic entering the intersection.

- A red arrow means turning traffic must stop.

- A yellow arrow indicates that the "protected" green arrow signal is about to turn to a regular circular green signal, circular red signal or red arrow signal.

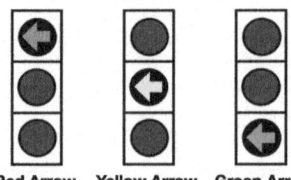

Red Arrow   Yellow Arrow   Green Arrow

Some traffic signals have a combination of "protected" turn arrow signals and "unprotected" circular signals based on traffic demand. At these intersections, both through traffic and turning traffic are controlled by circular signals if no arrow signal is displayed. When arrow and circular signals are both displayed, turning traffic is controlled by the arrow signals and through traffic is controlled by the circular signals. Below are examples of combination signal displays you may see.

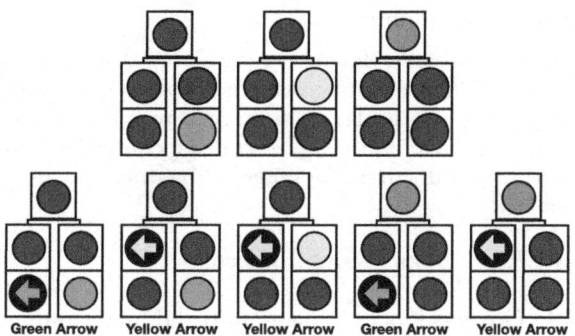

When approaching an intersection with a traffic light that has malfunctioned due to a power outage or some other problem, you should approach the intersection and proceed as though the intersection is controlled by a stop sign on all approaches to the intersection. This does not apply if a law enforcement officer or another authorized person is directing traffic, or if another type of traffic control device is in operation.

Flashing Signals

The flashing red signal has the same meaning as the stop sign: stop and do not proceed to move until you can enter the intersection without interfering with approaching traffic. The flashing yellow signal has the same meaning as a warning sign. Slow down and proceed with caution.

Left-Turn Traffic Signal Heads

The left-turn traffic signal head is designed to make it easier for drivers to know what to do when making a left turn. The traffic signal head will add a flashing yellow arrow. When the flashing yellow arrow is displayed, left turns are permitted but drivers must yield to oncoming traffic.

Below is what this style left-turn traffic signal head looks like and what drivers should do as the light changes:

 Solid Red Arrow: Stop. No turns are allowed.

 Solid Yellow Arrow: Prepare to stop.

 Flashing Yellow Arrow: Left turns are allowed, but first they must yield to oncoming traffic and pedestrians.

 Solid Green Arrow: Left turns allowed, and they do not need to yield to oncoming traffic and pedestrians. Proceed with caution.

Ramp Meter Traffic Signals:

A ramp meter signal is used to control traffic entering a freeway from an interchange entrance ramp.

When a ramp meter is displaying a circular red display, vehicles facing the red light must stop. When a ramp meter is displaying a circular green display, a vehicle facing the green display may proceed to merge onto the freeway. When the display is dark or not emitting a red or green display, a vehicle may proceed without stopping and enter the freeway by merging or yielding as normal conditions allow.

 Steady Red – Stop. Wait for Green

Steady Green – Proceed down ramp and merge onto freeway

Hybrid Beacons

Hybrid beacons may be used to control traffic at mid-block crosswalks and entrances to emergency response facilities. The beacons remain dark until activated by pedestrians or emergency response personnel. Once activated, the beacons will flash yellow for a few seconds, then go steady yellow and steady red for a few more seconds to allow moving vehicles to safely stop. Once vehicles have stopped, the beacons will remain steady red while pedestrians begin crossing or the emergency response vehicles begin exiting their facility. After several seconds, the beacons will begin flashing red, during which time vehicles are to remain stopped until the pedestrians or emergency response vehicles have cleared the intersection. After the pedestrians or emergency response vehicles have cleared the intersection, and after first coming to a complete stop, vehicles may begin moving while the beacons are flashing red.

Sequence for a Hybrid Beacon

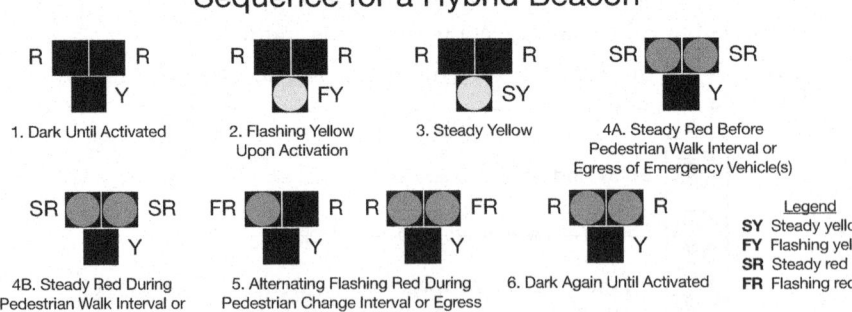

Traffic Signs

Shape and color make it possible to recognize the various kinds of highway signs at a glance.

Traffic signs are divided into three types:

1. Regulatory Signs

The eight-sided (or octagon) sign is the *stop* sign. The word "STOP" is printed in white on a red background. The octagonal shape is used for stop signs only. The stop sign is usually posted six to 50 feet from the intersection. When you approach this sign, the law requires you to come to a FULL stop. Do not proceed to move again until you are sure the way is clear.

When a stop sign, traffic light, flashing light or other traffic-control device requires a vehicle to stop at an intersection, the driver must stop at the appropriately marked stop line. If there is no stop line or marked crosswalk, the driver must stop before entering the intersection where he/she has a view of the intersecting street.

The *yield* sign is triangular shaped with the point at the bottom. This sign is red and white with the word "YIELD" in large letters at the top. When you approach the yield sign, you must slow down and yield the right of way. Your need to stop depends on the traffic on the intersecting street. To avoid interfering with that traffic, you must stop and wait for it to pass.

Rectangular and square-shaped signs, which are normally black and white or red and white, are also used to show speed limits and other regulations. These signs will also have messages such as "NO U-TURN" or "KEEP RIGHT EXCEPT TO PASS." Failure to obey these signs is unsafe as well as a violation of the traffic laws.

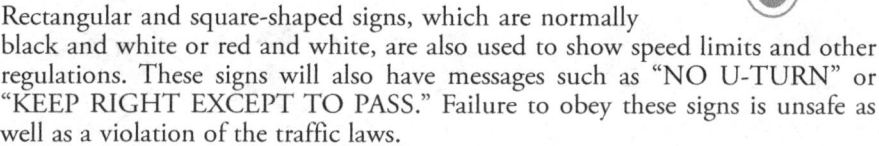

The *handicap parking* sign indicates that a space is reserved for persons who qualify for and are displaying a handicap license plate or a dashboard placard.

2. Warning Signs

The pennant–shaped yellow warning sign emphasizes, rather than replaces, the rectangular regulatory "DO NOT PASS" sign. The pennant is located on the left side of the road and points to the beginning of the no-passing zone (solid yellow line in your lane).

Diamond-shaped signs are also caution or warning signs. They are normally black on yellow, but when they are black on orange, they warn of conditions for construction or maintenance areas. When you see one of these signs, drive with extra care. One of the most important caution signs is the "STOP AHEAD" sign. It is placed far ahead of a stop sign when the driver's view of the stop sign is blocked by a curve or other objects. Diamond-shaped caution or warning signs that are orange with black messages warn about construction or maintenance areas. Highway work zones are covered in more detail in *Chapter 4 — Your Driving.*

Samples of caution or warning signs

A circular sign, with a black cross and the black letters "RR" on a yellow background, gives advance warning of a railroad crossing. When you see this sign, slow down. Stop if necessary to be sure you can safely clear the crossing.

At the railroad crossing itself is the railroad crossing crossbuck sign. The words "RAILROAD CROSSING" are printed in black on the white crosspieces. If there are multiple tracks at the crossing, they are shown on a sign below the crossbuck. You must stop at a railroad crossing whenever a flagman, signal or gate indicates an approaching train. You must remain stopped until the gate lifts or the signal or flagman indicates that it is safe to proceed. Take the time to check twice in each direction before crossing a railroad track.

Railroad Emergency Notification System sign

An example of the railroad Emergency Notification Sign is depicted in the red circle on the illustration below.

The five-sided (or pentagon) sign warns of a school zone or a school crossing. You should be especially watchful for children in these areas. In many school zones, the speed limit is reduced during certain school hours.

3. Guide/Informational Signs

Guide/informational signs give directions, routes, distances and indicate services.

Interstate, U.S. and N.C. highways are numbered and marked.

• Odd-numbered highways generally run north and south.

• Even-numbered highways generally run east and west.

• Route markers for U.S. highways are in the shape of a shield.

    • North Carolina route markers are diamond shaped.

    • N.C. secondary road signs are rectangular in shape.

    • Interstate highways are marked by  a red, white and blue shield.

    • Signs indicating a nearby hospital, Highway Patrol station or telephone are blue and white.

    • Guide signs, also rectangular in shape, may be green, brown or blue. They provide directions and distances. If you are lost, a mileage and directional sign can help you.

Do not endanger other drivers by stopping in the middle of the road to read a sign. When safe to do so, move to the shoulder of the road and wait until you have figured out where you are and which route you should take.

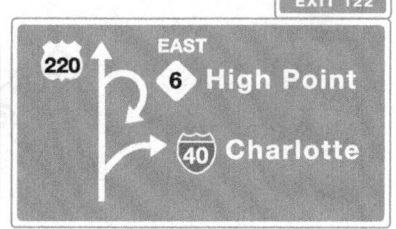

Regulatory Signs

No Bicycles   Left Turn Only   Thru & Left

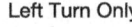

No Left Turn   Keep Left   Keep Right

No Right Turn   No U Turns   Double Left Turns

**The DO NOT STOP ON TRACKS sign reminds the driver
not to stop on the railroad track for any reason.**

Warning Signs

Signal Ahead	Merging Traffic	Lane Drop	Divided Highway
Cattle Crossing	Deer Crossing	Low Clearance	NO PASSING ZONE
Right Turn	Curve Right	Farm Machinery	Side Road
Divided Highway Ends	Two Way Traffic	Hill	Slippery When Wet
Bike Crossing	SOFT SHOULDER	Side Road	Cross Road
Winding Road	Stop Ahead	YIELD AHEAD	ROAD CLOSED 1500 FT
School	School Crossing	Railroad Crossing	

Pavement Markings

Yellow lines separate travel lanes moving in opposite directions. White lines separate travel lanes moving in the same direction. A yellow *skipped* or *broken line* is used as the center line on a two-lane, two-way road where passing with care is permitted in both directions. When continuous, double, solid, yellow lines are the center lines, you cannot cross them to pass in either direction. On a two-lane road, passing with care is permitted if the skipped-yellow line is in your lane.

Single, solid, white lines are used as right-edge lines along the roadway and for guiding traffic traveling in the same direction. Single, solid, yellow lines are used as left-edge lines on divided highways. If you see the reverse, you are traveling in the wrong direction. On certain multi-lane highways, a special center lane is reserved exclusively for two-way left-turn movements in both directions. The two-way left-turn lane must not be used for passing another vehicle or for the purpose of merging into traffic. The marking for this type of lane is shown by the diagram below.

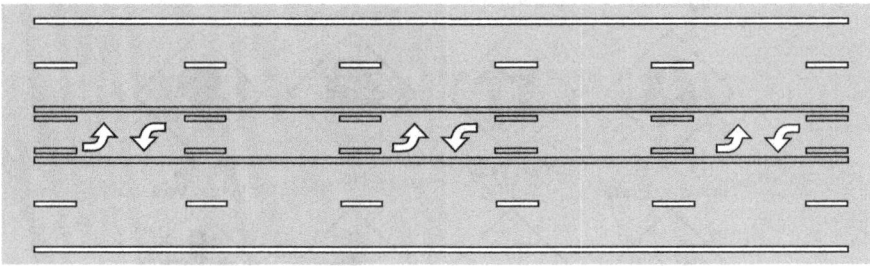

White and yellow pavement "markers" are reflective devices used in the pavement to improve the visibility of marking lines at night when the road is wet. Red markers indicate wrong-way movements for motorists. In some areas, blue reflective pavement markers on roadways indicate the location of nearby fire hydrants or water supplies for fire-fighting units.

Traffic Officers

Under special circumstances, an officer may be directing the flow of traffic. If so, obey the officer's hand signals instead of the normal traffic signals or signs. Most traffic officers signal drivers to stop by holding up one hand with the palm facing the vehicle and giving a long blast on the whistle. The officer signals drivers to start or to keep moving by motioning with the hand and giving a series of short blasts on the whistle. At night, the traffic officer may signal by using a flashlight.

Chapter 6
Sharing the Road

Our streets and highways are well traveled. Therefore, it is necessary that you, as a driver or pedestrian, know and practice the rules of the road. You should always be aware of the traffic around you and be prepared for emergency situations.

Bicycles

Bicycle riding is an important means of transportation, particularly for traveling to and from work and school. Because bicycles are vehicles, bicyclists must obey the same traffic laws as other drivers, this includes DWI laws.

Bicyclists, like any other vehicle, are entitled to use the full lane.

> **Like drivers, bicyclists must:**
> • Ride on the right side of the road;
> • Stop for stop signs and red lights; and
> • Give hand signals.

DRIVER'S MANUAL HAND SIGNALS — SIGNAL VARIATIONS CYCLISTS USE

LEFT TURN — LEFT TURN

RIGHT TURN — RIGHT TURN

STOP — STOP

Pass with Care

A bicyclist staying to the right in their lane is accommodating following drivers by making it easier to see when it is safe to pass, and easier to execute the pass. Drivers wishing to pass a bicyclist may do so only when there is abundant clearance and no oncoming traffic is in the opposing lane. The safest way to pass a bicyclist is to change lanes. To pass a cyclist lawfully, a driver must follow vehicle passing laws. Please see NCGS Sections 20-149 and 20-150.

Go with the Flow

It is especially important for bicyclists to go with the flow of traffic, NOT against the flow. Ride right, with the traffic, NOT facing traffic. Motorists often do not look in the direction of bicyclists riding the wrong way.

Be Visible

Visibility is important during both daylight hours and at night. During the daylight, avoid being obscured by other vehicles. At night, the law requires that a bicycle be equipped with a light on the front visible for a distance of at least 300 feet and a red light or reflector on the rear visible for a distance of at least 200 feet.

Bicyclists can be expected on all roads except where expressly prohibited. Bicycles are narrow and typically operate at the right of the lane, so they may be obscured and difficult to detect. Avoid the left cross, drive out and right hook types of potential collisions shown below.

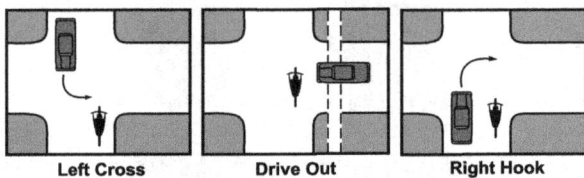

Left Cross   **Drive Out**   **Right Hook**

All bicycle riders and passengers under age 16 must wear an approved protective bicycle helmet and must be seated on a saddle seat.

A passenger weighing less than 40 pounds or less than 40 inches in height must be seated in a bicycle restraining seat.

For more information about bicycle riding skills write to:

NC Department of Transportation
Bicycle & Pedestrian Division
1552 Mail Service Center
Raleigh, NC 27699-1552
or call (919) 707-2600
www.ncdot.gov/bikeped

You as a Pedestrian

As drivers, we must watch out for pedestrians on the roadway. In cities, about two of every five persons killed by motor vehicle crashes are pedestrians; in rural areas, the rate is about one of every 10. Most of the pedestrians killed are children, elderly persons or those who have been drinking alcoholic beverages. When you are a pedestrian, do all you can to make yourself visible and to help drivers to prevent crashes.

Pedestrians should always:

• Walk on the left side of the road facing traffic;

• Wear or carry something white — do not assume that drivers can see you;

• Do everything you can to make yourself visible to drivers;

• Be ready to move out of the way in case a driver cannot see you; and

• At night, remember that it is more difficult for drivers to see you — use a flashlight.

Trucks and Other Vehicles

It is more difficult to drive a large truck than a passenger car for the following reasons:

• Heavy trucks cannot gain speed as quickly as cars, especially while traveling uphill. However, because of its large size, a tractor-trailer often appears to be traveling at a slower speed than it is;

• Large trucks require additional turning room because their rear wheels do not follow the path of their front wheels. When following a tractor-trailer, observe its turn signals before trying to pass. If it appears to be starting a left turn, check to see which way the driver is signaling before you attempt to pass; and

• Truck brakes create heat when the truck is traveling downhill. This condition requires additional stopping distance for the truck.

When driving beside large trucks or any large vehicle, the wind currents created by the larger vehicle may affect your steering. Give the truck plenty of room. When following large trucks, your vision may be blocked. Use caution while attempting to pass these vehicles.

No-Zones

Many motorists falsely assume that truckers can see the road better because they sit twice as high as the driver of a car. However, truckers still have serious blind

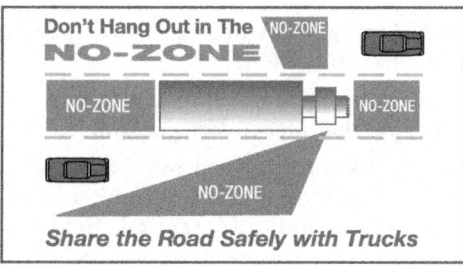

Share the Road Safely with Trucks

spots or NO-ZONES into which a car can disappear from view — up to 20 feet in front of the cab, on either side of the tractor-trailer, particularly alongside the cab, and up to 200 feet in the rear (see diagram).

Motorists lingering in the NO-ZONES hamper the trucker's ability to take evasive action to avoid a dangerous situation. An excellent rule of thumb for motorists sharing the road with a tractor-trailer is, *"if you can't see the truck driver in his side-view mirror, he can't see you."*

Recreational Vehicles and Trailers

- Most recreational vehicles, including motor homes, campers and travel trailers, are longer, higher and wider than passenger cars.

- Recreational vehicles and trailers accelerate and stop more slowly than cars and require more room for turning.

- Visibility is a major problem with recreational vehicles. Remember, that the closer you are as you approach a recreational vehicle, the more it will block your field of vision.

- Drivers of recreational vehicles can lose sight of you because their blind spots are much larger than those of cars.

When you approach a vehicle towing a trailer:

- Watch for any sway or possible hazards, such as crosswinds or slippery curves;

- Be aware that sudden braking might cause the trailer to jackknife; and

- Use extreme caution while passing a trailer and the towing vehicle — it may take you a half mile of clear roadway to safely pass.

Towing a trailer or boat requires special skill, as well as consideration on the part of each driver.

Motorcycles and Mopeds

Drivers share the road with motorcycles and mopeds, and they must be especially careful to look for them and to observe **these precautions**:

- Give the motorcyclist or moped rider the same right of way consideration as you would for the driver of any other vehicle;

- Motorcycles are entitled to the full width of their lane. To pass a motorcycle, you must change lanes and pass in the same manner as you would for a larger motor vehicle;

- A moped should travel using the right side of the lane. To pass a moped, you must stay at least two feet to the left; and

- You must leave any cyclist enough room when you pass so your vehicle's windstream cannot cause the rider to lose control.

Be especially watchful for motorcycles and mopeds while turning or changing lanes at intersections or entering the road from a driveway. Mopeds and motorcycles are difficult to see, and can be entirely hidden by your blind spots.

In many left-turn situations it is even more difficult to see a motorcycle or moped. Look out for motorcycles and mopeds, as well as other vehicles, before you turn, change lanes or proceed to move.

About two-thirds of motorcycle crashes in North Carolina involve a car. In most of these crashes, the driver of the car is at fault. The driver usually claims he or she did not see the motorcycle. Because the motorcycle offers little or no protection to the rider, the motorcyclist often is seriously injured or killed. Moped riders and all passengers are required to wear a helmet with a retention strap properly secured. The helmet must be a type that complies with Federal Motor Vehicle Safety Standard (FMVSS 218).

Motorcycles

Many small motorcycles do not accelerate rapidly and may not maintain speed going uphill or against a headwind. Stopping distances for motorcycles are also different. Most can stop more quickly than cars, but motorcycles stop more slowly when there is a second rider or when traveling on poor road surfaces where sudden braking could lead to a fall.

On the road, a cyclist traveling ahead of you could lose control when materials such as sand, gravel, wet leaves or water are on the pavement. Be aware of conditions that may cause a motorcyclist to fall. Watch out for motorcycles that wobble or jerk while starting to move, or cyclists who hesitate while making traffic decisions. These are signs of a beginning cyclist, so allow plenty of room.

Things to remember when you encounter a cyclist:

- Never crowd the motorcycle or moped. Following too closely does not allow enough reaction time in the case of an emergency;

- Allow a greater following distance when road surfaces are slippery. It is easier for the motorcycle or moped to become unstable because it has only two wheels in contact with the road surface;

- Always allow the cyclist plenty of room to maneuver, especially at railroad crossings or on rough and uneven roadways. If the crossing is rough or at an angle, the rider might need to slow down to cross; and

- Steel bridge expansion joints, metal grating on bridges and other metal surfaces are hazardous for cyclists. Leave plenty of space between yourself and the cyclist.

Mopeds

North Carolina law defines a moped as a vehicle with two or three wheels with a motor of no more than 50 cubic centimeters of piston displacement and no external shifting device. Legally, a moped's top speed cannot exceed 30 miles per hour. Although some mopeds on the market have top speeds higher than the 30 mph limit, they are illegal for use in North Carolina. Be sure you know a moped's size and maximum speed before you buy it. Otherwise, you may not be able to operate it legally.

In North Carolina you must be at least 16 years old to operate a moped on a public roadway or public vehicular area. No driver license is required. However, driving while impaired laws that apply to drivers of other motor vehicles also apply to moped operators. When riding a moped on a public roadway you must follow all the rules of the road.

In addition, you should follow the rules for riding a moped listed below:
• Stay out of traffic as much as possible;

• Try to find routes that are not traveled heavily;

• Keep your distance. In every situation leave a reasonable amount of space between you and the other vehicle;

• Keep to the right of your lane. Give yourself as much space as you can;

• Because you will probably be moving more slowly than the other traffic, other drivers will want to pass you. Stay out of their way, as much as possible;

• Do not share lanes with other vehicles;

• At an intersection, never squeeze between parked cars and moving traffic;

• Make sure other drivers can see you by wearing light or brightly colored clothing;

• If possible, install electric turn signals on your moped. Otherwise, be sure to use hand signals when you turn or stop;

• Look as far ahead as possible;

• Anytime you cross the path of traffic, slow down, stop and look carefully before you proceed to move;

• Be sure to look over your shoulder before you move into traffic and always be careful around parked cars;

• Protect your body. Wear protective clothing that covers your body and always wear shoes.

Registration of Mopeds *(Effective July, 2015)*
The North Carolina Division of Motor Vehicles requires all moped operators to register their vehicle with the DMV, and obtain a registration card and license plate, which must be displayed on the rear of the moped at all times.

Moped operators will be required to visit their local license plate agency for the registration process. The office locations can be found on the DMV website.

The cost of registering each moped is $24 annually. Durham ($15), Orange ($15), Randolph ($1) and Wake ($5) counties each charge an additional transit tax.

Operators must be 16 years of age or older and must have a valid N.C. driver license or N.C. ID card along with the moped manufacturer's certificate of origin (MCO). If an operator does not have an MCO for their vehicle, the operator can fill out an Affidavit of Facts for the Registration of a Moped form (MVR-58) to serve as proof of ownership.

Keeping the Road Litter-Free

In North Carolina, **littering is illegal**. When litter is thrown from or blown from a vehicle, the driver of the vehicle is held responsible. If convicted, the minimum fine is $250, and the maximum fine is $1,000. Any second or subsequent offense within three years after the date of a prior offense is punishable by a fine of not less than $500 nor more than $2,000, if convicted.

Adopt-A-Highway Program

The North Carolina Department of Transportation began its Adopt-A-Highway Program in April 1988. More than 7,000 volunteer groups have adopted about 15,000 miles of state-maintained roadsides, making North Carolina's Adopt-A-Highway program the largest of its kind in the nation.

To join the program, a civic, business, social or family group agrees to pick up litter at least four times a year along a two–mile section of state–maintained roadway. The Department of Transportation erects two signs identifying the adopted stretch of roadside and recognizing the group's contribution. In addition, NCDOT provides safety vests and training for each volunteer.

Volunteer groups are asked to recycle as much of the litter they pick up as possible. By recycling, Adopt-A-Highway volunteers are making an even greater contribution to their communities' environments.

The tremendous success of the Adopt-A-Highway program shows the great pride North Carolinians have in the beauty of their state. Please show your appreciation for these volunteers by obeying North Carolina's laws against littering.

For more information about the Adopt-A-Highway program, please visit the NCDOT Office of Beautification website at: ***www.ncdot.gov/beautification*** or call (919) 707-2970.

Chapter 7
How DMV Serves You

The Division of Motor Vehicles is responsible for promoting highway safety and serving the citizens of North Carolina through driver license, vehicle registration and vehicle inspection programs.

DMV Mobile Service Centers

Expanding and improving customer services to North Carolinians is a DMV goal. In keeping with that goal, DMV has equipped several mobile units with the latest driver license technology and turned them into mobile service centers.

You can do the following when visiting a MSC:

• Take the driver license knowledge and skills tests;

• Apply for an original driver license;

• Apply for a duplicate driver license;

• Take the commercial driver license knowledge test *(The skills test is not available at these sites.)*;

• Apply for a driver license renewal;

• Update your driver information; and

• Apply for a photo identification card.

Driver Records

You may obtain a copy of your driving record by visiting DMV headquarters or by visiting *MyNCDMV.gov*.

The Driver Privacy Protection Act Request Form (DL-DPPA-I), available at DMV Headquarters and on the DMV website, must be completed before your driving record can be obtained.

The form can be obtained at *MyNCDMV.gov*.

Fees (subject to change):

• $14 for certified copy of record (available online)

• $10 for non-certified full history (available online)

• $10 for non-certified record of three year history (not available online)

• $10 for non-certified record of seven year history (not available online)

• $13 for a copy of address history (not available online)

Three and seven year driver license record checks normally are used for insurance and employment purposes. A certified driver license record check usually is required for court appearances.

Make checks payable to NCDMV.

Mail form DL-DPPA-I along with a check for the appropriate amount to:
NC Division of Motor Vehicles
Driver License DR Unit
3113 Mail Service Center
Raleigh, NC 27697-3113

Vehicle Registration

A North Carolina driver license is required prior to titling/registering a vehicle in this State. Except for owners of exempt farm vehicles and exempt road construction equipment, every vehicle owner must register his or her motor vehicle with the Division of Motor Vehicles.

If you are a new North Carolina resident moving from out-of-state, your valid out-of-state driver's, along with your North Carolina Temporary Driving Certificate (TDC) will be required to title and register your vehicle.

See *MyNCDMV.gov* for more information on title and registration, available online services, fees, forms and license plate office hours and locations.

To register a vehicle:

• The owner must complete the required application forms; and

• Pay the appropriate title and registration fees.

Upon receipt of the application for motor vehicle registration:

• The DMV will issue a registration card, registration plate (license plate) and validation stickers to the owner;

• The registration card must be kept in the vehicle at all times and must always be available to show a law enforcement officer upon request;

• The license plate will show the unique number that has been assigned to the vehicle, the expiration date of the registration and that the vehicle is registered in North Carolina;

• The license plate must be displayed as required by law,

• Plastic license plate covers are prohibited. GS 20-63g.

How to change the address on your vehicle registration online:

To change the physical address on your vehicle registration, you can use our online duplicate vehicle registration card application at *MyNCDMV.gov*

You will need the following information:

• Vehicle license plate number

• Last five (5) characters of the vehicle title number

• Valid email address, so we can email your receipt

There is no charge to change your address online.

If your vehicle's registration is expired, you will need to renew your registration and change the address at the same time. The cost will be your regular renewal fee.

Change of Name or Address:

If you change your name or address, you must notify DMV within 60 days by writing to:

NC Division of Motor Vehicles
Vehicle Registration
3148 Mail Service Center
Raleigh, NC 27697.

Change of name /address forms are available at any local DMV vehicle registration office or on the DMV website at MyNCDMV.gov.

Remember these things when registering a vehicle:

* Before a vehicle can be registered in North Carolina, the DMV requires proper proof of ownership;

* For new vehicles, the manufacturer's certificate of origin is the official transfer document;

* If you purchase a used vehicle which has already been registered, you must present the certificate of title properly assigned by the former owner;

* To register a used vehicle for the first time in North Carolina, you must present the title from the state where the vehicle was formerly registered; and

* If the used vehicle is from a non-title state, you must present the current vehicle registration card with a properly notarized transfer of ownership on the back or a notarized bill of sale from the former owner and the former owner's proof of purchase.

* You must present a North Carolina Driver License or a North Carolina Identification Card. Valid driver licenses or identification cards issued by other states may be accepted for vehicle registrations with documentation of the following:

  * Military active duty stationed in North Carolina;

  * School enrollment in North Carolina;

  * Vehicle garaged in North Carolina for minimum of six months;

  * Court ordered sale of vehicle;

  * Vehicle is co-owned (one owner must have a North Carolina Driver License or ID);

  * Registration for motor home; or

  * Documented medical condition for an owner who would otherwise be eligible for a driver license or identification card.

  * Vehicle inspection must be valid

Insurance and Financial Responsibility

In addition to proof of ownership, North Carolina law requires that before a motor vehicle can be licensed, the owner must certify that the vehicle is covered by liability insurance. This can be in the form of a liability insurance policy issued from a company licensed to do business in the State of North Carolina, cash or bond deposited with the State Treasurer or a certificate of self-insurance for fleets of 25 or more vehicles. This law is enacted to ensure that the costs of a crash are paid by those who are responsible.

The minimum amount of liability insurance required is:

• $30,000 for injuries to any one person in a crash;

• $60,000 for all personal injuries in a crash; and

• $25,000 for all property damage in a crash.

• $750,000 for a commercial motor vehicle.

If the DMV is notified that a vehicle owner is operating a motor vehicle without proper liability insurance, the vehicle's license plate could be revoked for 30 days unless proof of continuous insurance coverage is provided. If a lapse did occur, the registered owner could be subject to a fine or penalty.

North Carolina law requires the owner of every registered vehicle to maintain continuous liability insurance as long as the vehicle has a valid license plate. Liability insurance policies are effective at 12:01 a.m. on the date of issuance, remain in effect for a period of six months and expire at 12:01 a.m., six months later. This information is also indicated on the declaration page of the policy issued by the insurance company. North Carolina does not honor a grace period. A grace period is an agreement between the Insured and the insurance company only.

Additional information regarding liability insurance requirements or options available for registered owners who may have had a lapse, may be found on our website or by calling (919) 715-7000.

Vehicle Registration Renewal

Within 90 days prior to the registration expiration, all self-propelled vehicles are required to receive a safety or safety and emission inspection to renew their registration.

Upon expiration of vehicle registration, the vehicle's owner must renew the registration by submitting a renewal application and paying the appropriate registration fee. Upon payment of the appropriate fee, DMV will issue license plate stickers to indicate the new period of valid registration and vehicle inspection. DMV uses a staggered vehicle registration system. This method of registration staggers registration renewals over 12 months of the year.

To avoid a fine or penalty, surrender a vehicle's valid license plate prior to the termination or cancellation of liability insurance.

Transfer of a Motor Vehicle

When a motor vehicle owner wishes to transfer his interest in the vehicle to someone else, reassignment of ownership should be made by using section "A" on side two of the certificate of title. In order for the transfer to be valid, the reassignment must be made in the presence of a Notary Public and the actual delivery of the vehicle to the new owner must be made. A current inspection is required within the last 12 months prior to the sale if a registration plate will be requested.

Transfer of License Plates

License plates can be transferred from one vehicle to another of the same category provided ownership is in the same name and insurance coverage has been continuous.

Replacement of Lost Title or Registration Card

If a certificate of title is lost or stolen, a duplicate title may be obtained by completing an application for duplicate title and paying the appropriate fee. A duplicate title cannot be issued until 15 days after the application and fee are received by the DMV. Application forms are available at any local DMV vehicle registration office or on the DMV website at *MyNCDMV.gov.*

A duplicate registration card can be obtained with payment of the appropriate fee. Application forms are available at any local DMV vehicle registration office or on the DMV website at *MyNCDMV.gov.*

Tag & Tax Together

North Carolina law now requires vehicle owners to pay for registration renewal of license tags and vehicle property taxes at the same time. Drivers used to pay for tags and taxes separately. The "Tag & Tax Together" program requires one payment for both bills. Both tag renewals and tax payments must be paid in full to renew a vehicle's annual registration.

Yearly combined notices are mailed to current vehicle owners and contain registration and inspection information about the vehicle as well as tax information from counties and other taxing jurisdictions.

DMV is not involved in establishing the value of a vehicle for property tax purposes. The local county assessment office determines the tax based on the make and model of the registered vehicle.

This law covers all motor vehicles except:

• Vehicles exempt from registration by North Carolina law;

• Manufactured homes;

• Mobile classrooms and offices;

• Semi-trailers registered on a multi-year basis; and

• Motor vehicles owned or leased by public service companies.

• Park Model Trailers;

• Mopeds

How do I pay?

Paying your vehicle's Tag & Tax together has never been easier! We offer three convenient ways:

Pay online.

Visit *MyNCDMV.gov*.

Visit your local License Plate Agency.

Most offices offer services from 9 a.m. to 5 p.m. Monday through Friday.

The following office provides customer service from 8 a.m. until 5 p.m. Monday through Friday of each week:

Raleigh - 1100 New Bern Avenue

The following office only provides instant titles for all customers and renewal services for customers with disabilities from 8 a.m. until 5 p.m. Monday through Friday of each week:

Charlotte - 6016 Brookshire Boulevard

Pay by mail.

P.O. Box 29620
Raleigh, NC 27626

Vehicle Emissions & Safety Inspection

All motor vehicles registered in North Carolina must be inspected annually. DMV License & Theft Bureau oversees the vehicle inspection process. The objective of vehicle inspections is to ensure vehicles registered in North Carolina are maintained properly.

In North Carolina a vehicle must pass the required safety-only inspection or safety and emissions inspection before it can be registered and the license tag renewed.

The vehicle inspection can be performed at any licensed inspection station located throughout the state. For an up to date list of inspection station locations, please visit *MyNCDMV.gov*.

Inspections may be performed up to 90 days prior to the vehicle's registration (license tag) expiration date. A vehicle that fails inspection is entitled to be re-inspected at the same station within 60 days without paying another inspection fee.

Exemptions

If your vehicle is light-duty, gasoline powered, three years old or less, and registered in one of the 48 emissions counties, it may be exempt from an emissions inspection under General Statute 20-183.2

Vehicles with less than 70,000 miles and within the "three most recent model years" will receive a safety only inspection.

You can find the model year for your vehicle on your registration card under the column labeled "YEAR".

The law exempts emission testing for vehicles that are registered in or sold in North Carolina if they are within the three most recent model years and have less than 70,000 miles on the odometer.

The law only exempts the emission portion of the annual inspection for vehicles in the counties where emissions inspections are required on 1996 and newer vehicles.

Window Tinting

Vehicles with after-factory window tinting will be charged an additional fee of $10 as part of the vehicle inspection. The allowable light transmittance for tinted windows is no less than 35%. If you have any questions about window tinting, please contact your local law enforcement.

NORTH CAROLINA
DRIVER HANDBOOK

North Carolina Division of Motor Vehicles

Motor vehicle laws and fees are subject to change by the North Carolina General Assembly. Revised April 2018. Current fees effective January 1, 2016.

The North Carolina Driver Handbook is available online at **MyNCDMV.gov** under License and ID.

Division of Motor Vehicles
Driver and Vehicle Services Section
North Carolina Transportation

Physical Location: (DMV Headquarters)
(Licenses are not issued at this location).
1100 New Bern Avenue, Raleigh, NC 27697

Mailing Address:
3123 Mail Service Center
Raleigh, NC 27697-3123

MyNCDMV.gov

Made in the USA
Columbia, SC
03 February 2026